STUDY GUIDE AND WORKING PAPERS CHAPTERS 1-12

COLLEGE ACCOUNTING

Tenth Edition

Jeffrey Slater

North Shore Community College

PEARSON

Prentice Hall

Upper Saddle River, New Jersey 07458

VP/Editorial Director: Jeff Shelstad
Executive Editor: Wendy Craven
Project Manager: Kerri Tomasso
Associate Director, Manufacturing: Vincent Scelta
Production Editor & Buyer: Carol O'Rourke
Printer/Binder: Courier Kendallville

10 9 8 7 6 5 4 3 2 1
ISBN 0-13-228639-4

Contents

Week 3 Homework
Read Chapter 1 & 2 Review PP 1 & 2

Chapter 2 Homework = Group B Problems on pg 68 thru 70
form on 36 thru 43

INTRODUCTION TO ACCOUNTING CONCEPTS AND PROCEDURES

1

SELF-REVIEW QUIZ 1-1

GRACIE RYAN REAL ESTATE

	ASSETS			=	LIABILITIES	+	OWNER'S EQUITY
	Cash	+	Computer Equipment	=	Accounts Payable	+	Gracie Ryan, Capital
TRANSACTION 1	17000						17000
NEW BALANCE	17000			=			17000
TRANSACTION 2	- 600		600				
NEW BALANCE	16,400		600	=			17,000
TRANSACTION 3			800		800		
ENDING BALANCE	16,400	+	1,400	=	800	+	17,000
			17,800	=	17,800		

SELF-REVIEW QUIZ 1-2

Tanning Company
Balance Sheet
November 30 2008

ASSETS						LIABILITIES AND OWNER'S EQUITY						
Cash	18	0	0	0	00	Liabilities						
Office Equipment	31	0	0	0	00	Accounts Payable	40	0	0	0	00	
Assets	49	0	0	0	00	Owner's Equity						
						A. Tanning (Capital)	9	0	0	0	00	
						Total Liabilities +						
						Owners equity	49	0	0	0	00	

SELF-REVIEW QUIZ 1-3

B. BING CO.

	ASSETS			= LIABILITIES	+ OWNER'S EQUITY				
	Cash +	Accounts Receivable +	Cleaning Equipment	= Accounts Payable	+ B. Bing, Capital	− B. Bing Withd.	+ Revenue	− Expenses
Beg. Balance	$10,000	$2,500	$6,500	= $1,000	+ $11,800	− $800	+ $9,000	− $2,000
1.	+4000	2500					+4000	
Balance	14,000	2500	6500	= 1000	11,800	800	13000	2000
2.		−1000					6000	
Balance	14,000	8500	6500	= 1000	11,800	800	19,000	200
3.				+125				+125
Balance	14,000	8500	6500	= 1125	11,800	−800	19,000	2125
4.	−500					−500		
Balance	12,500	8500	6500	= 1125	11,800	−1300	19,000	2125
5.	+1000	−1000						
Ending Balance	14,500 +	1500 +	6500	= 1125	+ 11,800	− 1300	+ 19,000	− 2125

28,500 = 28,500

SELF-REVIEW QUIZ 1-4

(1)

Rusty Realty
Income Statement
November 30 2008

Revenues:								
Commissions Earned						1 5 0 0	00
Operating Expense:							
Rent Expense			2 0 0	00			
Advertising Expense			1 5 0	00			
Salaries Expense			9 0	00	4 4 0	00	
Net Income					1 0 6 0	00	

(2)

Rusty Realty
Statement of Owner's Equity
Novemember 30 2008

R. Rusty Capital, November 1 2008					5 0 0 0	00
Net Income of November		1 0 6 0	00		
Less: Withdrawals		1 0 0	00		
Increase in Capital				9 6 0	00
R. Rusty, Capital November 30, 2008				5 9 6 0	00

(3)

Rusty Realty
Balance Sheet
November 30 2008

ASSETS						LIABILITIES AND OWNER'S EQUITY					
Cash		4	0	0	0	00	Liabilities						
Accounts Receivable		1	3	7	0	00	Accounts Payable			9	0	0	00
Store Furniture		1	4	9	0	00							
							Owner's Equity						
							R. Rusty, Capital		5	9	6	0	00
Total Assets		6	8	6	0	00	Total Liabilities +						
							Owner's equity		6	8	6	0	00

The net income from the income statement is used to help build the statement of owner's equity

The new figure for capital from the statement of owner's equity is used as the capital figure on the balance sheet.

FORMS FOR DEMONSTRATION PROBLEM

(A)

MICHAEL BROWN, ATTORNEY AT LAW

	ASSETS			= LIABILITIES +	OWNER'S EQUITY			
	Cash	+ Accounts Receivable	+ Office Equipment	= Accounts Payable	+ M. Brown, Capital	− M. Brown, Withd.	+ Legal fees	− Expenses
1.	+16000				16000			
Balance	16000				16000			
2.	−600		600					
Balance	15400		600		16000			
3.			1000	1000				
Balance	15400		1600	1000	16000			
4.	2000						2000	
Balance	17400		1600	1000	16000		2000	
5.	−800							800
Balance	16600		1600	1000	16000		2000	800
6.		1000					1000	
Balance	16600	1000	1600	1000	16000		3000	800
7.	−1200							1200
Balance	15400	1000	1600	1000	16000		3000	2000
8.	−500					500		
Balance	14900	1000	1600	1000	16000	500	3000	2000
9.	+500	−500						
Ending Balance	15400	500	1600	1000	16000	500	3000	2000

17500 = 17500

DEMONSTRATION PROBLEM (CONTINUED)

B-1

MICHAEL BROWN, ATTORNEY AT LAW
INCOME STATEMENT
FOR MONTH ENDED JUNE 30, 200X

Revenues:				
Legal fees:			3 0 0 0	00
Operating Expense				
Salaries Expense	8 0 0 00			
Rent Expense	1 2 0 0 00			
		2 0 0 0	00	
Total Operating Expense				
Net income			1 0 0 0	00

B-2

MICHAEL BROWN, ATTORNEY AT LAW
STATEMENT OF OWNER'S EQUITY
FOR MONTH ENDED JUNE 30, 200X

Michael Brown Capital June 1 2008			6 0 0 0	00
Net Income for June	1 0 0 0 00			
Less: Withdrawals	5 0 0 00			
Increase in Capital			5 0 0	00
Michael Brown Capital June 30, 2008			6 5 0 0	00

B-3

MICHAEL BROWN, ATTORNEY AT LAW
BALANCE SHEET
JUNE 30, 200X

ASSETS			LIABILITIES AND OWNER'S EQUITY		
Cash	5 4 0 0 00		Liabilities		
Acct. Rec.	5 0 0 00		Acct Payable	1 0 0 0	00
office Equipment	1 6 0 0 00		Owner's Equity		
Total Assets	7 5 0 0 00		M. Brown Capital	6 5 0 0	00
			Total Liabilities +		
			Owner's equity	7 5 0 0	00

CHAPTER 1
FORMS FOR CLASSROOM DEMONSTRATION PROBLEMS SET A OR SET B

1. A. _____ A
    B. _____ OE
    C. _____ L
    D. _____ A
    E. _____ A
    F. _____ A

2. A. _____ _____ _____
    B. _____
    C. _____

3. A. _____
    B. _____

4. _____
    _____
    _____

5. _____
    _____
    _____
    _____
    _____

6. _____
    _____
    _____
    _____

7. A. _____
    B. _____
    C. _____
    D. _____

8. A. _____
    B. _____
    C. _____
    D. _____
    E. _____
    F. _____
    G. _____
    H. _____

9. A. _____
    B. _____
    C. _____
    D. _____

FORMS FOR EXERCISES

1-1.

    A. _____

    B. _____

    C. _____

1-2.

	ASSETS	=	LIABILITIES	+	OWNER'S EQUITY
A.					
B.					
C.					

1-3.

JINGLE CLEANERS
BALANCE SHEET
NOVEMBER 30, 200X

ASSETS			LIABILITIES AND OWNER'S EQUITY		

EXERCISES (CONTINUED)

1-4.

	ASSETS			=	LIABILITIES	+		OWNER'S EQUITY		
	Cash	+	Accounts Receivable	+	Computer Equipment	=	Accounts Payable	+	B. Bell Capital	−	B. Bell Withd.	+	Revenue	−	Expenses
A.										
B.										
C.										
D.										
E.										
F.										
G.										
Ending Balance										

EXERCISES (CONTINUED)

1-5.

(A)

FRENCH REALTY
INCOME STATEMENT
FOR MONTH ENDED JUNE 30, 200X

(B)

FRENCH REALTY
STATEMENT OF OWNER'S EQUITY
FOR MONTH ENDED JUNE 30, 200X

(C)

FRENCH REALTY
BALANCE SHEET
JUNE 30, 200X

ASSETS   LIABILITIES AND OWNER'S EQUITY

END OF CHAPTER PROBLEMS

PROBLEM 1A-1 OR PROBLEM 1B-1

BETTY'S DOG GROOMING CENTER

	ASSETS			= LIABILITIES	+	OWNER'S EQUITY
	Cash	+	Equipment	= Accounts Payable	+	Betty Sullivan, Capital
TRANSACTION A	19,000					19,000
NEW BALANCE	19,000					19,000
TRANSACTION B	-3000		3000			
NEW BALANCE	16,000		3000			19,000
TRANSACTION C	—		2000	2000		
NEW BALANCE	16,000		5000	2000		19,000
TRANSACTION D	-300			-300		
ENDING BALANCE	15,700		5000	1700		19,000
			20,700	20,700		

PROBLEM 1A-2 OR PROBLEM 1B-2

BLUE'S INTERNET SERVICE
BALANCE SHEET
SEPTEMBER 30, 200X

ASSETS					LIABILITIES AND OWNER'S EQUITY					
Cash	12	0	0	0	00	Liabilities				
Equipment	16	0	0	0	00	Accounts Payable	20	0	0	0	00
Building	40	0	0	0	00					
						Owner's Equity				
Total Assets	68	0	0	0	00	Blues Capital	48	0	0	0	00
						Owner's Equity	68	0	0	0	00

PROBLEM 1A-3 OR PROBLEM 1B-3

RICK FOX
TYPING SERVICE

	ASSETS			= LIABILITIES +	OWNER'S EQUITY				
	Cash	+ Accounts Receivable	+ Office Equipment	= Accounts Payable	+ R. Fox, Capital	– R. Fox, Withd.	+ Typing Revenue	– Expenses
A.	10,000				10,000			
BALANCE	10,000				10,000			
B.			4000	4000				
BALANCE	10,000		4000	4000	10,000			
C.	500						500	
BALANCE	10,500		4000	4000	10,000		500	
D.		2100					2100	
BALANCE	10,500	2100	4000	4000	10,000		2600	
E.	-350							350
BALANCE	10,150	2100	4000	4000	10,000		2600	350
F.	-210							210
BALANCE	9,940	2100	4000	4000	10,000		2600	560
G.	900	2100	4000	900	10,000		2600	900
BALANCE	9040	2100	4000	4900	10,000		2600	1460
H.	-400					400		
ENDING BALANCE	9640	2100	4000	4900	10,000	400	2600	1460

15,740   15,740

PROBLEM 1A-4 OR PROBLEM 1B-4

(A)

WEST STENCILING SERVICE
INCOME STATEMENT
FOR MONTH ENDED JUNE 30, 200X

Revenues:												
Stenciling Fees										3 0 0 0	00	
Operating Expense												
Advertising Expense			1 1 0	00								
Relay Expense			2 5	00								
Travel Expense			2 5 0	00								
Supplies Expense			1 9 0	00								
Rent Expense			2 5 0	00								
Total Operating Expense			8 2 5	00								
Net Income									2 1 7 5	00		

(B)

WEST STENCILING SERVICE
STATEMENT OF OWNER'S EQUITY
FOR MONTH ENDED JUNE 30, 200X

J. West, Capital June 1 200X									1 2 0 0	00	
Net Income for June			2 1 7 5	00								
Less Withdrawal for June			3 0 0	00								
Increase in Capital for June								1 8 7 5	—		
J West Capital June 31 200X								3 0 7 5	—		

PROBLEM 1A-4 OR PROBLEM 1B-4 (CONCLUDED)

WEST STENCILING SERVICE
BALANCE SHEET
JUNE 30, 200X

ASSETS					LIABILITIES AND OWNER'S EQUITY				
Cash	2	3	00	—	Liabilities				
Account Receivable		4	00	00	Accounts Payable		3	10	—
Equipment		6	85	—					
					Owner's Equity				
					J. West Capital	3	0	75	—
Total Assets	3	3	85	—					
					Owner's Equity	3	3	85	—

PROBLEM 1A-5 OR PROBLEM 1B-5

TOBEY'S CATERING SERVICE

	ASSETS			= LIABILITIES +	OWNER'S EQUITY			
	Cash +	Accounts Receivable +	Equipment =	Accounts Payable +	J. Tobey, Capital -	J. Tobey, Withd. +	Catering Revenue -	Expenses
10/25	20,000				20,000			
BALANCE	20,000				20,000			
10/27	-700		700					
BALANCE	19,300		700		20,000			
10/28			1000	1000				
BALANCE	19,300		1000	1000	20,000			
10/29	-600		1700	600				
BALANCE	18,700		1700	1600	20,000			
11/1	+2400						2400	1690
BALANCE	21,100		1700	1600	20,000		2400	1690
11/5	-600	300					300	1000
BALANCE	20,410	300	1700	1600	20,000		2700	1000
11/8	+100	-100						
BALANCE	20,610	200	1700	1600	20,000		2700	1690
11/10	-10						2700	-10
BALANCE	20,450	200	1700	1600	20,000		2700	750
11/15							2700	750
11/17	-90					90		
BALANCE	20,360	200	1700	1600	20,000	90	2700	750
11/20	+1800						1800	750
BALANCE	22,160	200	1700 + 400	1600 + 400	20,000	90	4500	750
11/25	22,160	200	2100	2000	20,000	90	4500	1000
BALANCE	22,160	200	2100	2000	20,000	90	4500	1350
11/28	-400			-400				400
BALANCE	21,760	200	2100	1600	20,000	90	4500	1750
END. BAL.	21,760	200	2100	1600	20,000	90	4500	1750

24060 = 24060

PROBLEM 1A-5 OR PROBLEM 1B-5 (CONTINUED)

(B)

TOBEY'S CATERING SERVICE
BALANCE SHEET
OCTOBER 31, 200X

ASSETS					LIABILITIES AND OWNER'S EQUITY				
Cash	18	7 0 0	00		Liabilities				
Equipment	1	7 0 0	00		Accounts Payable		1 4 0 0	00	
Total Assets	20	4 0 0	00		Owner's Equity				
					T. Catering Service		19 0 0 0	00	
					Total liabilitie and				
					Owner's Equity		20 4 0 0	—	

(C)

TOBEY'S CATERING SERVICE
INCOME STATEMENT
FOR MONTH ENDED NOVEMBER 30, 200X

Revenue						
Catering Revenue					4 5 0 0	00
Operating Expense						
Salaries Expense		6 9 0	00			
Phone Bill Expense		6 0	00			
Rent Expense		6 0 0	00			
Supply Expense		4 0 0	00			
Total Operating Expense					1 7 5 0	00
Net Income					2 7 5 0	00

PROBLEM 1A-5 OR PROBLEM 1B-5 (CONTINUED)

(D)

TOBEY'S CATERING SERVICE
STATEMENT OF OWNER'S EQUITY
FOR MONTH ENDED NOVEMBER 30, 200X

Tobey Catering Capital November 1 2008						24	4 0 0	00
Net Income for November		2 7 5 0	—			2 7 5 0	—
Less: Withdrawals		9 0	—			9 0	—
						2 6 6 0	00
Tobey Catering Capital November 31 2008						24 0 6 0	00

(E)

TOBEY'S CATERING SERVICE
BALANCE SHEET
NOVEMBER 30, 200X

ASSETS				LIABILITIES AND OWNER'S EQUITY			
Cash	21 7 6 0	—	Liabilities			
Account Receivable	2 0 0	—	Accounts Payable	24 4 0 0	00
Equipment	2 1 0 0	—			
			Owner's Equity		
Total Assets	24 0 6 0	—	Tobey's Capital	22 6 6 0	—
			Less Withdrawals	9 0	—
			Owner Equity	24 0 6 0	00

CHAPTER 1
SUMMARY PRACTICE TEST:
INTRODUCTION TO ACCOUNTING CONCEPTS AND PROCEDURES

Part 1 Instructions

Fill in the blank(s) to complete the statement.

1. _____ is the recording function of the accounting process.
2. Assets = _Liabilities_ + Owner's Equity
3. The owner's current investment or equity in the assets of a business is called _Capital_ .
4. A list of assets, liabilities, and owner's equity as of a particular date is reported on a _Income_ _statement_ .
5. _____ create an outward or potential outward flow of assets.
6. Revenue earned on account creates an asset entitled _Accounts_ _Receivable_ .
7. _____ record personal expenses that are not related to the business. They are a subdivision of owner's equity.
8. The _____ _____ reports how well a business performs for a period of time.
9. The _Statement_ _of_ _Owner's_ _Equity_ is a report that shows changes in capital.
10. The ending figure for capital from the statement of owner's equity is placed on the _____ _____ .

Part II Instructions

Answer true or false to the following statements.

1. Business transactions are recorded in monetary terms.
2. Assets less Liabilities equals Owner's Equity.
3. Revenue is an asset.
4. Capital means cash.
5. Bookkeeping is 50 percent of accounting.
6. The balance sheet lists assets, revenue, and owner's equity.
7. The balance sheet shows where we are now for a specific period of time.
8. Revenue creates an outward flow of assets.
9. Expenses are a subdivision of owner's equity.
10. Withdrawals are the only subdivision of owner's equity.
11. Withdrawals are listed on the income statement.
12. Revenue is a subdivision of owner's equity.

13. Revenues and withdrawals are listed on the income statement.
14. The income statement helps update the statement of owner's equity, and the statement of owner's equity helps update the balance sheet.
15. Withdrawals are listed on the statement of owner's equity.

Part III Instructions

In column B, record the appropriate code(s) that result from recording the transaction in column A.

1. Increase in assets
2. Decrease in assets
3. Increase in liabilities
4. Decrease in liabilities

5. Increase in capital
6. Increase in revenues
7. Increase in expenses
8. Increase in withdrawals

COLUMN A	COLUMN B
1. EXAMPLE: Jim Murray invested $1,000 in his business.	1,5
2. Bought equipment on account for $100.	_____
3. Paid salaries of $50	_____
4. Bought additional equipment for $500 cash.	_____
5. Paid rent expense of $50.	_____
6. Received $5,000 in cash from revenue earned.	_____
7. Paid heat expense of $15.	_____
8. Earned revenue of $500 that will not be received until next month.	_____
9. Paid amount owed on equipment previously purchased on account.	_____
10. Paid for cleaning supplies expense, $15.	_____
11. Customers paid $10 of amount previously owed.	_____
12. Bought additional equipment of $1,000, half paid in cash and half charged.	_____
13. Charged customer $100 for services performed.	_____
14. Jim paid home phone bill from the company's cash.	_____
15. Advertising expense incurred but not to be paid until next month.	_____

CHAPTER 1 SOLUTIONS TO SUMMARY PRACTICE TEST

Part I

1. bookkeeping
2. liabilities
3. capital
4. balance sheet

5. expenses
6. Accounts Receivable
7. withdrawals
8. income statement

9. statement of owner's equity
10. balance sheet

Part II

1.	true	**6.**	false	**11.**	false
2.	true	**7.**	false	**12.**	true
3.	false	**8.**	false	**13.**	false
4.	false	**9.**	true	**14.**	true
5.	false	**10.**	false	**15.**	true

Part III

1.	1,5	**6.**	1,6	**11.**	1,2
2.	1,3	**7.**	7,2	**12.**	1,2,3
3.	7,2	**8.**	1,6	**13.**	1,6
4.	1,2	**9.**	4,2	**14.**	8,2
5.	7,2	**10.**	7,2	**15.**	7,3

CONTINUING PROBLEM FOR CHAPTER 1

SANCHEZ COMPUTER CENTER

	ASSETS				=	LIABILITIES	+	OWNER'S EQUITY			
	Cash +	Supplies +	Computer Shop Equipment +	Office Equipment =		Accounts Payable	+	Freedman, Capital +	Freedman, – Withdrawals +	Revenue –	Expenses
a											
BALANCE											
b											
BALANCE											
c											
BALANCE											
d											
BALANCE											
e											
BALANCE											
f											
BALANCE											
g											
BALANCE											
h											
BALANCE											
i											
BALANCE											
j											
END BAL.											

SANCHEZ COMPUTER CENTER
INCOME STATEMENT
FOR THE MONTH ENDED JULY 31, 200X

SANCHEZ COMPUTER CENTER
STATEMENT OF OWNER'S EQUITY
FOR MONTH ENDED JULY 31, 200X

SANCHEZ COMPUTER CENTER
BALANCE SHEET
JULY 31, 200X

ASSETS		LIABILITIES AND OWNER'S EQUITY

2

DEBITS AND CREDITS: ANALYZING AND RECORDING BUSINESS TRANSACTIONS

SELF-REVIEW QUIZ 2-1

1. _____ F _____   4. _____ T _____
2. _____ F _____   5. _____ F _____
3. _____ T _____

SELF-REVIEW QUIZ 2-2

A. 1.	2.	3.	4.	5.
Accounts Affected	Category	↑↓	Rules	T Account Update

B. 1.	2.	3.	4.	5.
Accounts Affected	Category	↑↓	Rules	T Account Update

C. 1.	2.	3.	4.	5.			
Accounts Affected	Category	↑↓	Rules	T Account Update			

D. 1.	2.	3.	4.	5.			
Accounts Affected	Category	↑↓	Rules	T Account Update			

E. 1.	2.	3.	4.	5.			
Accounts Affected	Category	↑↓	Rules	T Account Update			

SELF-REVIEW QUIZ 2-3

Cash	111
4,500	300
2,000	100
1,000	1,200
300	1,300
	2,600

Accounts Payable	211
300	700

Salon Fees	411
	3,500
	1,000

Accounts Receivable	121
1,000	300

Pam Jay, Capital	311
	4,000

Rent Expense	511
1,200	

Salon Equipment	131
700	

Pam Jay, Withdrawals	321
100	

Salon Supplies Exp.	521
1,300	

Salaries Expense	531
2,600	

Name _____ Class _____ Date _____

(1)

_____
_____
_____

(2)

_____
_____
_____

(3)

_____

_____

_____

(4)

_____

_____

_____

FORMS FOR DEMONSTRATION PROBLEM

(1,2,3)

Advertising Expense   511

Gas Expense   512

Salaries Expense   513

Telephone Expense   514

Accounts Payable   211

Mel Free, Capital   311

Mel Free, Withdrawals   312

Delivery Fees Earned   411

Cash   111

Accounts Receivable   112

Office Equipment   121

Delivery Trucks   122

FORMS FOR DEMONSTRATION PROBLEM (CONTINUED)

(4)

MEL'S DELIVERY SERVICE
TRIAL BALANCE
JULY 31, 200X

	Dr.	Cr.

(5A)

MEL'S DELIVERY SERVICE
INCOME STATEMENT
FOR MONTH ENDED JULY 31, 200X

FORMS FOR DEMONSTRATION PROBLEM (CONTINUED)

(5B)

MEL'S DELIVERY SERVICE
STATEMENT OF OWNER'S EQUITY
FOR MONTH ENDED JULY 31, 200X

(5C)

MEL'S DELIVERY SERVICE
BALANCE SHEET
JULY 31, 200X

ASSETS		LIABILITIES AND OWNER'S EQUITY

CHAPTER 2
FORMS FOR CLASSROOM DEMONSTRATION EXERCISES SET A OR SET B

1.

2. A. _____

B. _____

C. _____

D. _____

E. _____

F. _____

G. _____

3.

4. _____

_____

_____

_____

_____

_____

_____

_____

_____

5. A. _____

B. _____

C. _____

D. _____

E. _____

F. _____

G. _____

H. _____

I. _____

J. _____

K. _____

FORMS FOR EXERCISES

2-1

_____
_____
_____
_____
_____
_____
_____
_____
_____
_____
_____
_____
_____
_____
_____
_____
_____
_____
_____
_____

2-2

1 Accounts Affected	2. Category	3 ↑ ↓	4 Rules	5 T-Account Update

2-3

Account	Category	↑ ↓	Financial Statement

EXERCISES (CONTINUED)

2-4.

	Dr.	Cr.
A.	8	1
B.		
C.		
D.		
E.		
F.		
G.		
H.		
I.		

2-5.

(1)

HALL'S CLEANERS
INCOME STATEMENT
FOR MONTH ENDED JULY 31, 200X

(2)

HALL'S CLEANERS
STATEMENT OF OWNER'S EQUITY
FOR MONTH ENDED JULY 31, 200X

EXERCISES (CONTINUED)

(3)

HALL'S CLEANERS
BALANCE SHEET
JULY 31, 200X

ASSETS					LIABILITIES AND OWNER'S EQUITY				

END OF CHAPTER PROBLEMS

PROBLEM 2A-1 OR PROBLEM 2B-1

Accounts Affected	Category	Inc. Dec.	Rules	T-Account Update
A.	Cash / Owner's Capital	↑		Cash 2500 / Capital 2500
B.	Equipment / Acct Payable			Equipment 900 / Acct. Payable 900
C.	Acct Payable / Expense			Acct Payable 250 / Expense 250
D.	Cash / Revenue			Cash 1100 / Earned Revenue 1100
E.	Acct Payable / Earned Revenue			Acct Payable 700 / Earned Revenue 700
F.	Cash / Withdrawals			Cash 275 / Withdrawals 275

PROBLEM 2A-2 OR PROBLEM 2B-2

Cash   111
20,000	
1200	200
	600
	400

Jill Jay, Withdrawals   312
	200

Office Equipment   121
6000	

Consulting Fees Earned   411
	1200

Accounts Payable   211
	6000
	500
400	

Advertising Expense   511
600	

Jill Jay, Capital   311
	20,000

Rent Expense   512
500	

PROBLEM 2A-3 OR PROBLEM 2B-3

(A)

Cash	111
10,000	4000
4000	310
2000	50
	1000
16,000	4960.
11,040.	

Accounts Payable	211
	2,000
	2000.

Fees Earned	411
	4,000
	4,000
	8000

Accounts Receivable	112
2000	
2000	

Mike Frank, Capital	311
	10,000
	10,000

Rent Expense	511
310	
310	

Office Equipment	121
2000	
4000	
6000	

Mike Frank, Withdrawals	312
1000	
1000	

Utilities Expense	512
50	
50	

(B)

MIKE'S WINDOW WASHING SERVICE
TRIAL BALANCE
MAY 31, 200X

		Dr.	Cr.
Cash	111	11 040 00	
Acct. Receivable		2 000 00	
Equipment		6 000 00	
Acct Payable			2 000 00
Mike Frank Capital			10 000 00
Mike Frank withdrawals		1 000 00	
Fee Earned			8 000 00
Rent Expense		310 00	
Utilities Expense		50 00	
Totals		20 000 00	20 000 00

PROBLEM 2A-4 OR PROBLEM 2B-4

(A)

GRACIE LANTZ, ATTORNEY AT LAW
INCOME STATEMENT
FOR MONTH ENDED MAY 31, 200X

Revenues:										
Revenue from Legal fees							8	8	0 0	00
Operating Expense:										
Rent Expense			3	0 0	00					
Salaries Expense			4	0 0	00					
Utilities Expense			1	0 0	00					
Total operating Expense:								8 0 0	00
Net Income							8	0 0 0	00

(B)

GRACIE LANTZ, ATTORNEY AT LAW
STATEMENT OF OWNER'S EQUITY
FOR MONTH ENDED MAY 31, 200X

Gracie Lantz Capital for May 1 200X						4	0 0 0	00
Net Income for May		8	0 0 0	00				
Less: Withdrawals		2	0 0	00				
						6	0 0 0	00	*
Gracie Lantz Capital for May 31 200X						10	0 0 0	00

PROBLEM 2A-4 OR 2B-4 (CONCLUDED)

(C)

GRACIE LANTZ, ATTORNEY AT LAW
BALANCE SHEET
MAY 31, 200X

ASSETS				LIABILITIES AND OWNER'S EQUITY			
Cash	6 0 0 0	00		Liabilities & Owner's Equity			
Acct Receivable	2 4 0 0	00		Liabilities			
office Equipment	2 4 0 0	00		Acct Payable	2 0 0 0	00
				Salaries Payable	6 0 0	00
Total Assets	10 8 0 0	00		Owner's Equity			
				Gracie Lantz Capital	10 0 0 0	00
				Gracie Lantz Capital			
				MAY 31 200X	10 8 0 0	00

PROBLEM 2A-5 OR PROBLEM 2B-5

(1,2,3)

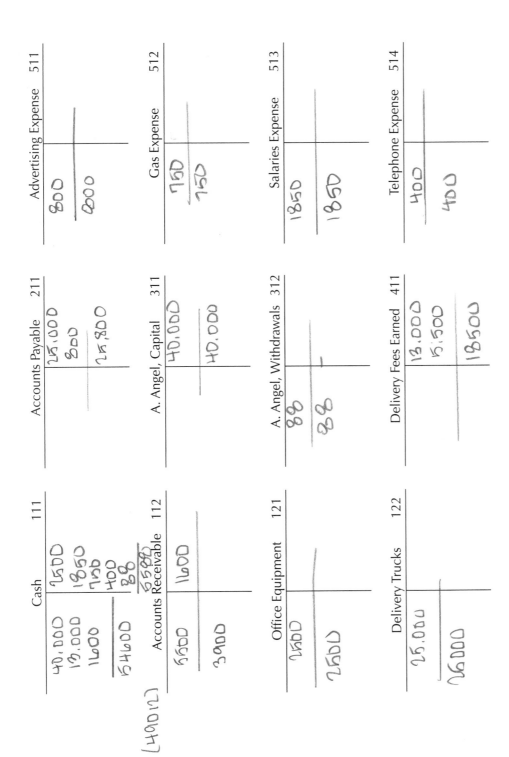

(4)

ANGEL'S DELIVERY SERVICE
TRIAL BALANCE
MARCH 31, 200X

	Dr.	Cr.
Cash	49 012 00	
Account Receivable	3 900 00	
Office Equipment	2 500 00	
Delivery Truck	25 000 00	
Accounts Payable		25 800 00
A. Angel Capital		40 000 00
A. Angel Withdrawals	888 00	
Delivery Fees Earned		18 500 00
Advertising Expense	800 ✓	
Gas Expense	750 ✓	
Salaries Expense	1 850	
Telephone Expense	400 ✓	
Totals	84 300 00	84 300 00

(5A)

ANGEL'S DELIVERY SERVICE
INCOME STATEMENT
FOR MONTH ENDED MARCH 31, 200X

Revenues:		
Delivery Fees Earned		18 500 00
Operating Expenses:		
Advertising Expense	800 ✓	
Gas Expense	750 ✓	
Salaries Expense	1 850 ✓	
Telephone Expense	400 ✓	
		3 800 ✓
		14 700 00

PROBLEM 2A-5 OR 2B-5 (CONCLUDED)

(5B)

ANGEL'S DELIVERY SERVICE
STATEMENT OF OWNER'S EQUITY
FOR MONTH ENDED MARCH 31, 200X

Angel's Captal									40	0	0	0	00
March 31 200X													
Net Income for March		14	7	0	0	00							
Less: Withdrawals				8	8	00							
Angel Capital									14	6	1	2	00
for March 31, 200X									54	6	1	2	00

(5C)

ANGEL'S DELIVERY SERVICE
BALANCE SHEET
MARCH 31, 200X

ASSETS						LIABILITIES AND OWNER'S EQUITY				
Cash	49	0	1	2	—	Liabilities:				
Accounts Receivable	3	9	0	0	—	Acct Payable	25	8	0	0	—
Office Equipment	2	5	0	0	—					
Delivery Truck	25	0	0	0	—	Owner's Equity:				
						Angel Capital	54	6	1	2	—
total Assets	80	4	1	2	—	Total liabilities				
						and Owner's Equity	80	4	1	2	—

CHAPTER 2
SUMMARY PRACTICE TEST:
DEBITS AND CREDITS: ANALYZING AND RECORDING
BUSINESS TRANSACTIONS

Part I Instructions

Fill in the blank(s) to complete the statement.

1. _____ accumulate information in a book called the ledger.
2. The left side of any T account is called the _____ _____.
3. Assets are increased by _____ .
4. The process of balancing an account involves _____ .
5. Transaction analysis charts are an aid in recording _____ _____ .
6. The _____ _____ _____ indicates the names and numbering system of accounts.
7. A _____ is a group of accounts.
8. A _____ _____ is an informal report that lists accounts and their balances.
9. Withdrawals are increased by _____ .
10. The income statement, statement of owner's equity, and balance sheet may be prepared from a _____ _____ .
11. Cash, Accounts Receivable, and Equipment are examples of _____ .
12. Increasing expenses ultimately cause owner's equity to _____ .
13. An increase in rent expense is a _____ by the rules of debits and credits.
14. A debit to one asset and a credit to another asset for the same transaction reflect a _____ in assets.
15. The category of accounts payable is a/an _____ .

Part II Instructions

Abby Lane opened a taxi company. From the following chart of accounts, indicate in column B (by account number) which account (s) will be debited or credited as related to the transaction in column A.

Name _____ Class _____ Date _____

Chart of Accounts

ASSETS	LIABILITIES	EXPENSES
10 Cash	50 Accounts Payable	80 Advertising
20 Accounts Receivable		90 Gas
30 Equipment	OWNER'S EQUITY	100 Salaries
40 Taxi	60 A. Lane, Capital	110 Telephone
	62 A. Lane, Withdrawals	
	REVENUE	
	70 Taxi Fees Earned	

COLUMN A   **COLUMN B**

		DEBIT(S)	CREDIT(S)
1.	EXAMPLE: Abby Lane invested $25,000 in the taxi company.	10	60
2.	Purchased a taxi on account for $40,000.	_____	_____
3.	Bought equipment on account for $6,000.	_____	_____
4.	Advertising bill received, but not paid til next month.	_____	_____
5.	Abby paid home telephone bill from company checkbook, $20.	_____	_____
6.	Collected $100 in cash from daily taxi fees earned.	_____	_____
7.	Customer charged a taxi ride of $10.	_____	_____
8.	Received partial payment for Transaction #7 of $5.	_____	_____
9.	Paid business telephone bill, $32.	_____	_____
10.	Purchased additional equipment for cash, $550.	_____	_____
11.	Paid taxi driver salaries of $150.	_____	_____
12.	Drove customer on account to local train station for $6.	_____	_____
13.	Received $5 from customer who hired taxi for ride across town.	_____	_____
14.	Collected from past charged revenue, $15.	_____	_____
15.	Bought office equipment on account for $110.	_____	_____

Part III Instructions

Answer true or false to the following statements.

1. There are debit and credit columns found on the three financial statements.
2. A trial balance could balance but be wrong.
3. Withdrawals are listed on the credit column of the trial balance.
4. Double entry bookkeeping results in a system where the sum of all the debits is equal to the sum of all the credits.
5. The ledger is numbered like a textbook.

6. Withdrawals are always increased by credits.

7. An expense could create a liability.

8. A shift in assets means the total of assets must change.

9. The rules of debit and credit are constantly changing.

10. The transaction analysis chart is a teaching device.

11. The chart of accounts makes locating and identifying accounts easier.

12. The left side of any account is a credit.

13. A debit means all accounts are decreasing.

14. Financial statements are prepared from a trial balance.

15. The statement of owner's equity is prepared before the income statement.

16. Liabilities increase by credits.

17. Footings aid in balancing accounts.

18. Withdrawals are listed on the income statement.

19. The balance sheet contains the old figure for capital.

20. Think of a credit as always meaning something good.

CHAPTER 2
SOLUTIONS TO SUMMARY PRACTICE TEST

Part I

1. accounts
2. debit side
3. debits
4. footings
5. business transactions
6. chart of accounts
7. ledger (general)
8. trial balance
9. debits
10. trial balance
11. assets
12. decrease
13. debit
14. shift
15. liability

Part II

	Debit	Credit		Debit	Credit		Debit	Credit
1.	10	60	6.	10	70	11.	100	10
2.	40	50	7.	20	70	12.	20	70
3.	30	50	8.	10	20	13.	10	70
4.	80	50	9.	110	10	14.	10	20
5.	62	10	10.	30	10	15.	30	50

Part III

1. false
2. true
3. false
4. true
5. false
6. false
7. true
8. false
9. false
10. true
11. true
12. false
13. false
14. true
15. false
16. true
17. true
18. false
19. false
20. false

CONTINUING PROBLEM FOR CHAPTER 2

Cash	1000
Bal. 3,850	

Accounts Receivable	1020

Supplies	1030
Bal. 250	

Computer Shop Equipment	1080
Bal. 1,200	

Freedman, Withdrawals	3010
Bal. 100	

Office Equipment	1090
Bal. 600	

Accounts Payable	2000
	335 Bal.

Freedman, Capital	3000
	4,500 Bal.

Utilities Expense	5030
Bal. 85	

Service Revenue	4000
	1,650 Bal.

Advertising Expense	5010

Rent Expense	5020
Bal. 400	

Postage Expense	5070

Phone Expense	5040

Supplies Expense	5050

Insurance Expense	5060

SANCHEZ COMPUTER CENTER
TRIAL BALANCE
AUGUST 31, 200X

		Dr.	Cr.

SANCHEZ COMPUTER CENTER
INCOME STATEMENT
FOR THE TWO MONTHS ENDED AUGUST 31, 200X

SANCHEZ COMPUTER CENTER
STATEMENT OF OWNER'S EQUITY
FOR THE TWO MONTHS ENDED AUGUST 31, 200X

SANCHEZ COMPUTER CENTER
BALANCE SHEET
AUGUST 31, 200X

ASSETS		LIABILITIES AND OWNER'S EQUITY	

BEGINNING THE ACCOUNTING CYCLE: JOURNALIZING, POSTING, AND THE TRIAL BALANCE

3

SELF-REVIEW QUIZ 3-1

PAGE 1

Date	Account Titles and Description	PR	Dr.	Cr.

LOWE'S REPAIR SERVICE
GENERAL JOURNAL

PAGE 1 (cont'd)

Date	Account Titles and Description	PR	Dr.	Cr.

SELF-REVIEW QUIZ 3-2

CLARK'S WORD PROCESSING SERVICES
GENERAL JOURNAL

PAGE 1

Date 200x		Account Titles and Description	PR		Dr.					Cr.			
May	1	Cash		10	0	0	0	00					
		Brenda Clark, Capital							10	0	0	0	00
		Initial investment of cash by owner											
	1	Word Processing Equipment		6	0	0	0	00					
		Cash							1	0	0	0	00
		Accounts Payable							5	0	0	0	00
		Purchase of equip. from Ben Co.											
	1	Prepaid Rent		1	2	0	0	00					
		Cash							1	2	0	0	00
		Rent paid in advance (3 months)											
	3	Office Supplies			6	0	0	00					
		Accounts Payable								6	0	0	00
		Purchase of supplies on acct. from Norris											
	7	Cash		3	0	0	0	00					
		Word Processing Fees							3	0	0	0	00
		Cash received for services rendered											
	13	Office Salaries Expense			6	5	0	00					
		Cash								6	5	0	00
		Payment of office salaries											
	18	Advertising Expense			2	5	0	00					
		Accounts Payable								2	5	0	00
		Bill received but not paid from Al's News											
	20	Brenda Clark, Withdrawals			6	2	5	00					
		Cash								6	2	5	00
		Personal withdrawal of cash											
	22	Accounts Receivable		5	0	0	0	00					
		Word Processing Fees							5	0	0	0	00
		Billed Morris Co. for fees earned											

CLARK'S WORD PROCESSING SERVICES
GENERAL JOURNAL

PAGE 2

Date 200x		Account Titles and Description	PR			Dr.				Cr.			
May	27	Office Salaries Expense			6	5	0	00					
		Cash								6	5	0	00
		Payment of office salaries											
	28	Accounts Payable		2	5	0	0	00					
		Cash							2	5	0	0	00
		Paid half the amount owed Ben Co.											
	29	Telephone Expense			2	2	0	00					
		Cash								2	2	0	00
		Paid telephone bill											

PARTIAL LEDGER OF CLARK'S WORD PROCESSING SERVICE

CASH   ACCOUNT NO. 111

Date	Explanation	Post Ref.	Debit	Credit	Balance	
					Debit	Credit

ACCOUNTS RECEIVABLE   ACCOUNT NO. 112

Date	Explanation	Post Ref.	Debit	Credit	Balance	
					Debit	Credit

OFFICE SUPPLIES   **ACCOUNT NO. 114**

Date		Explanation	Post Ref.	Debit	Credit	Balance	
						Debit	Credit

PREPAID RENT   **ACCOUNT NO. 115**

Date		Explanation	Post Ref.	Debit	Credit	Balance	
						Debit	Credit

WORD PROCESSING EQUIPMENT   **ACCOUNT NO. 121**

Date		Explanation	Post Ref.	Debit	Credit	Balance	
						Debit	Credit

ACCOUNTS PAYABLE   **ACCOUNT NO. 211**

Date		Explanation	Post Ref.	Debit	Credit	Balance	
						Debit	Credit

BRENDA CLARK, CAPITAL   ACCOUNT NO. <u>311</u>

Date	Explanation	Post Ref.	Debit	Credit	Balance Debit	Balance Credit

BRENDA CLARK, WITHDRAWALS   ACCOUNT NO. <u>312</u>

Date	Explanation	Post Ref.	Debit	Credit	Balance Debit	Balance Credit

WORD PROCESSING FEES   ACCOUNT NO. <u>411</u>

Date	Explanation	Post Ref.	Debit	Credit	Balance Debit	Balance Credit

OFFICE SALARIES EXPENSE   ACCOUNT NO. <u>511</u>

Date	Explanation	Post Ref.	Debit	Credit	Balance Debit	Balance Credit

ADVERTISING EXPENSE   **ACCOUNT NO. 512**

Date	Explanation	Post Ref.	Debit	Credit	Balance Debit	Balance Credit

TELEPHONE EXPENSE   **ACCOUNT NO. 513**

Date	Explanation	Post Ref.	Debit	Credit	Balance Debit	Balance Credit

SELF-REVIEW QUIZ 3-3

1. _____

_____

_____

2. P. 4

Date	Account Titles and Description	PR	Dr.			Cr.		

FORMS FOR DEMONSTRATION PROBLEM
(A, B)

ABBY'S EMPLOYMENT AGENCY
GENERAL JOURNAL

PAGE 1

Date	Account Titles and Description	PR	Dr.	Cr.

FORMS FOR DEMONSTRATION PROBLEM (CONTINUED)

GENERAL LEDGER OF ABBY'S PLACEMENT AGENCY

CASH ACCOUNT NO. 111

Date	Explanation	Post Ref.	Debit	Credit	Balance Debit	Balance Credit

ACCOUNTS RECEIVABLE ACCOUNT NO. 112

Date	Explanation	Post Ref.	Debit	Credit	Balance Debit	Balance Credit

SUPPLIES ACCOUNT NO. 131

Date	Explanation	Post Ref.	Debit	Credit	Balance Debit	Balance Credit

EQUIPMENT ACCOUNT NO. 141

Date	Explanation	Post Ref.	Debit	Credit	Balance Debit	Balance Credit

FORMS FOR DEMONSTRATION PROBLEM (CONTINUED)

ACCOUNTS PAYABLE   ACCOUNT NO. 211

Date		Explanation	Post Ref.	Debit	Credit	Balance	
						Debit	Credit

A. TODD, CAPITAL   ACCOUNT NO. 311

Date		Explanation	Post Ref.	Debit	Credit	Balance	
						Debit	Credit

A. TODD, WITHDRAWALS   ACCOUNT NO. 321

Date		Explanation	Post Ref.	Debit	Credit	Balance	
						Debit	Credit

EMPLOYMENT FEES EARNED   ACCOUNT NO. 411

Date		Explanation	Post Ref.	Debit	Credit	Balance	
						Debit	Credit

FORMS FOR DEMONSTRATION PROBLEM (CONTINUED)

WAGE EXPENSE   ACCOUNT NO. <u>511</u>

Date		Explanation	Post Ref.	Debit	Credit	Balance	
						Debit	Credit

TELEPHONE EXPENSE   ACCOUNT NO. 521

Date		Explanation	Post Ref.	Debit	Credit	Balance	
						Debit	Credit

ADVERTISING EXPENSE   ACCOUNT NO. 531

Date		Explanation	Post Ref.	Debit	Credit	Balance	
						Debit	Credit

FORMS FOR DEMONSTRATION PROBLEM (CONTINUED)

ABBY'S EMPLOYMENT AGENCY
TRIAL BALANCE
MARCH 31, 200X

		Dr.		Cr.	

CHAPTER 3
FORMS FOR CLASSROOM DEMONSTRATION EXERCISES SET A OR SET B

1. A. _____   E. _____
   B. _____   F. _____
   C. _____   G. _____
   D. _____   H. _____
                               I. _____

2. A. _____
   B. _____
   C. _____

3. _____
   _____

4.

LEE CO.
TRIAL BALANCE
OCTOBER 31, 200X

	Dr.	Cr.

5.

FORMS FOR EXERCISES

3-1.

Date	Account Titles and Description	PR	Dr.	Cr.

3-2.

Date		Account Titles and Description	PR		Dr.				Cr.		

EXERCISES (CONTINUED)

3-3.

Date		Account Titles and Description	PR	Dr.	Cr.
200X					
April	6	Cash		15 0 0 0 —	
		A. King, Capital			15 0 0 0 —
		Cash investment			
	14	Equipment		9 0 0 0 —	
		Cash			4 0 0 0 —
		Accounts Payable			5 0 0 0 —
		Purchase of Equipment			

CASH — ACCOUNT NO. 111

Date	Explanation	Post Ref.	Debit	Credit	Balance Debit	Balance Credit

EQUIPMENT — ACCOUNT NO. 121

Date	Explanation	Post Ref.	Debit	Credit	Balance Debit	Balance Credit

ACCOUNTS PAYABLE — ACCOUNT NO. 211

Date	Explanation	Post Ref.	Debit	Credit	Balance Debit	Balance Credit

A. KING, CAPITAL — ACCOUNT NO. 311

Date	Explanation	Post Ref.	Debit	Credit	Balance Debit	Balance Credit

EXERCISES (CONTINUED)

3-4.

(A)
PAGE 1

Date	Account Titles and Description	PR	Dr.	Cr.

(B)

ACCOUNTS RECEIVABLE   **ACCOUNT NO. 111**

Date	Explanation	Post Ref.	Debit	Credit	Balance Debit	Balance Credit

PREPAID RENT   **ACCOUNT NO. 112**

Date	Explanation	Post Ref.	Debit	Credit	Balance Debit	Balance Credit

EXERCISES (CONTINUED)

EQUIPMENT   ACCOUNT NO. 121

Date		Explanation	Post Ref.	Debit	Credit	Balance	
						Debit	Credit

ACCOUNTS PAYABLE   ACCOUNT NO. 211

Date		Explanation	Post Ref.	Debit	Credit	Balance	
						Debit	Credit

J. LOWE, CAPITAL   ACCOUNT NO. 311

Date		Explanation	Post Ref.	Debit	Credit	Balance	
						Debit	Credit

J. LOWE, WITHDRAWALS   ACCOUNT NO. 312

Date		Explanation	Post Ref.	Debit	Credit	Balance	
						Debit	Credit

FEES EARNED   ACCOUNT NO. 411

Date		Explanation	Post Ref.	Debit	Credit	Balance	
						Debit	Credit

SALARIES EXPENSE   ACCOUNT NO. 511

Date		Explanation	Post Ref.	Debit	Credit	Balance	
						Debit	Credit

EXERCISES (CONTINUED)

(C)

LOWE COMPANY
TRIAL BALANCE
JULY 31, 200X

		Dr.		Cr.	

3-5.

SUNG CO.
TRIAL BALANCE
MARCH 31, 200X

		Dr.		Cr.	

3-6.

		Dr.		Cr.	

END OF CHAPTER PROBLEMS

PROBLEM 3A-1 OR PROBLEM 3B-1

PETE'S FITNESS CENTER
GENERAL JOURNAL

PAGE 1

Date		Account Titles and Description	PR	Dr.	Cr.
2008 11	1	Prepaid Rent	114	7 0 0 0 00	
		Cash	111		7 0 0 0 00
2008 11	6	Equipment Fitness	121	4 4 0 0 00	
		Acct. Payable	211		4 4 0 0 00
2008 11	12	Fitness Supplies	116	5 0 0 00	
		Cash			5 0 0 00
2008 11	14	Cash	111	1 7 0 0 00	
		Fitness Fees Earned	411		1 7 0 0 00
2008 11	20	Pete Ret. Withdrawals	312	7 0 0 00	
		Cash	111		7 0 0 00
2008 11	21	Advertising Expense	511	2 0 0 00	
		Acct. Payable	211		2 0 0 00
2008 11	25	Cleaning Expense	514	1 1 0 00	
		Cash	111		1 1 0 00
2008 11	28	Salaries Expense	512	6 0 0 00	
		Cash	111		6 0 0 00
2008 11	29	Acct Receivable	112	1 9 0 0 00	
		Fitness Fees Earned	411		1 9 0 0 00
2008 11	30	Acct Payable	211	2 2 0 0 00	
		Cash	111		2 2 0 0 00

PROBLEM 3A-1 OR PROBLEM 3B-1 (CONCLUDED)

PETE'S FITNESS CENTER
GENERAL JOURNAL

PAGE 2

Date	Account Titles and Description	PR	Dr.	Cr.

PROBLEM 3A-2 OR PROBLEM 3B-2
(A, B)

BETTY'S ART STUDIO
GENERAL JOURNAL

PAGE 1

Date		Account Titles and Description	PR	Dr.	Cr.
2008 6	1	Cash ✓	111	12 000 00	
		Betty Rice, Capital ✓	311		12 000 00
2008 6	1	Prepaid Rent ✓	114	1 200 00	
		Cash ✓	111		1 200 00
2008 6	3	Equipment ✓	131	600 00	
		Acct. Payable ✓	211		600 00
2008 6	5	Cash ✓	111	900 00	
		Art Fees Earned ✓	411		900 00
2008 6	8	Art Supplies ✓	121	400 00	
		Cash ✓	111		400 00
2008 11	9	Acct Receivable ✓	112	2 100 00	
		Art Fees Earned ✓	411		2 100 00
2008 6	10	Salaries Expense ✓	521	600 00	
		Cash ✓	111		600 00
2008 6	15	Betty Rice Withdrawals ✓	312	200 00	
		Cash ✓	111		200 00
2008 6	18	Electrical Expense	511	140 00	
		Cash ✓	111		140 00
2008 6	19	Telephone Expense	531	210 00	
		Cash ✓	111		210 00

PROBLEM 3A-2 OR PROBLEM 3B-2 (CONTINUED)

GENERAL LEDGER OF BETTY'S ART STUDIO

CASH   ACCOUNT NO. 111

Date	Explanation	Post Ref.	Debit	Credit	Balance Debit	Balance Credit
			12000 00			
					12000 00	
				1200 00	10800 00	
			900 00		11700 00	
				400 00	11300 00	
				600 00	10700 00	
				200 00	10500 00	
				140 00	10360 00	
				210 00	10150 00	

ACCOUNTS RECEIVABLE   ACCOUNT NO. 112

Date	Explanation	Post Ref.	Debit	Credit	Balance Debit	Balance Credit
			2100 00		2100 00	

PREPAID RENT   ACCOUNT NO. 114

Date	Explanation	Post Ref.	Debit	Credit	Balance Debit	Balance Credit
			1200 00		1200 00	

ART SUPPLIES   ACCOUNT NO. 121

Date	Explanation	Post Ref.	Debit	Credit	Balance Debit	Balance Credit
			400 00		400 00	

PROBLEM 3A-2 OR PROBLEM 3B-2 (CONTINUED)

EQUIPMENT   ACCOUNT NO. 131

Date	Explanation	Post Ref.	Debit	Credit	Balance Debit	Balance Credit
			600 00		600 00	

ACCOUNTS PAYABLE   ACCOUNT NO. 211

Date	Explanation	Post Ref.	Debit	Credit	Balance Debit	Balance Credit
				600 00		600 00

BETTY RICE, CAPITAL   ACCOUNT NO. 311

Date	Explanation	Post Ref.	Debit	Credit	Balance Debit	Balance Credit
				12 000 00		12 000 00

BETTY RICE, WITHDRAWALS   ACCOUNT NO. 312

Date	Explanation	Post Ref.	Debit	Credit	Balance Debit	Balance Credit
			200 00		200 00	

PROBLEM 3A-2 OR PROBLEM 3B-2 (CONTINUED)

ART FEES EARNED   **ACCOUNT NO. 411**

Date	Explanation	Post Ref.	Debit	Credit	Balance Debit	Balance Credit
				2 0 0 00		2 0 0 00
				2 1 0 0 00		2 1 0 0 00
						3 0 0 00

ELECTRICAL EXPENSE   **ACCOUNT NO. 511**

Date	Explanation	Post Ref.	Debit	Credit	Balance Debit	Balance Credit
			1 4 0 00		1 4 0 00	

SALARIES EXPENSE   **ACCOUNT NO. 521**

Date	Explanation	Post Ref.	Debit	Credit	Balance Debit	Balance Credit
			6 0 0 00		6 0 0 00	

TELEPHONE EXPENSE   **ACCOUNT NO. 531**

Date	Explanation	Post Ref.	Debit	Credit	Balance Debit	Balance Credit
			2 1 0 00		2 1 0 00	

PROBLEM 3A-2 OR PROBLEM 3B-2 (CONCLUDED)

(C)

BETTY'S ART STUDIO
TRIAL BALANCE
JUNE 30, 200X

	Dr.				Cr.		
Cash	10 1 5 0	00					
Acct Receivable	2 1 0 0	00					
Prepaid Rent	1 2 0 0	00					
Art Supplies	4 0 0	00					
Equipment	6 0 0	00					
Acct Payable					6 0 0	00	
Betty Rice Capital				12 0 0 0	00		
Betty Rice Withdrawals	2 0 0	00					
Art Fees Earned				3 0 0 0	00		
Electrical Expense	1 4 0	00					
Salaries Expense	6 0 0	00					
Telephone Expense	2 1 0	—					
Total	15 6 0 0	00		15 6 0 0	00		

PROBLEM 3A-3 OR PROBLEM 3B-3
(A, B)

A. FRENCH'S PLACEMENT AGENCY
GENERAL JOURNAL

P. 1

Date		Account Titles and Description	PR	Dr.	Cr.
2008 June	1	Cash	111	9 0 0 0 00	
		A. French Capital	311		9 0 0 0 00
	1	Equipment	141	2 0 0 0 00	
		Acct Payable	211		2 0 0 0 00
	3	Acct Receivable	112	1 6 0 0 00	
		Placement Fees Earned	411		1 6 0 0 00
	5	A. French Withdrawals	312	1 0 0 00	
		Cash	111		1 0 0 00
	7	Wage Expense	521	3 0 0 00	
		Cash	111		3 0 0 00

PROBLEM 3A-3 OR PROBLEM 3B-3 (CONTINUED)

GENERAL LEDGER OF A. FRENCH'S PLACEMENT AGENCY

CASH   ACCOUNT NO. 111

Date	Explanation	Post Ref.	Debit	Credit	Balance	
					Debit	Credit

ACCOUNTS RECEIVABLE   ACCOUNT NO. 112

Date	Explanation	Post Ref.	Debit	Credit	Balance	
					Debit	Credit

SUPPLIES   ACCOUNT NO. 131

Date	Explanation	Post Ref.	Debit	Credit	Balance	
					Debit	Credit

EQUIPMENT   ACCOUNT NO. 141

Date	Explanation	Post Ref.	Debit	Credit	Balance	
					Debit	Credit

PROBLEM 3A-3 OR PROBLEM 3B-3 (CONTINUED)

ACCOUNTS PAYABLE   ACCOUNT NO. 211

Date	Explanation	Post Ref.	Debit	Credit	Balance Debit	Balance Credit

A. FRENCH, CAPITAL   ACCOUNT NO. 311

Date	Explanation	Post Ref.	Debit	Credit	Balance Debit	Balance Credit

A. FRENCH, WITHDRAWALS   ACCOUNT NO. 312

Date	Explanation	Post Ref.	Debit	Credit	Balance Debit	Balance Credit

PLACEMENT FEES EARNED   ACCOUNT NO. 411

Date	Explanation	Post Ref.	Debit	Credit	Balance Debit	Balance Credit

PROBLEM 3A-3 OR PROBLEM 3B-3 (CONTINUED)

WAGE EXPENSE   ACCOUNT NO. 511

Date	Explanation	Post Ref.	Debit	Credit	Balance Debit	Balance Credit

TELEPHONE EXPENSE   ACCOUNT NO. 521

Date	Explanation	Post Ref.	Debit	Credit	Balance Debit	Balance Credit

ADVERTISING EXPENSE   ACCOUNT NO. 531

Date	Explanation	Post Ref.	Debit	Credit	Balance Debit	Balance Credit

PROBLEM 3A-3 OR PROBLEM 3B-3 (CONCLUDED)

(C)

A. FRENCH'S PLACEMENT AGENCY
TRIAL BALANCE
JUNE 30, 200X

		Dr.	Cr.

CHAPTER 3
SUMMARY PRACTICE TEST:
BEGINNING THE ACCOUNTING CYCLE: JOURNALIZING,
POSTING, AND THE TRIAL BALANCE

1. A _____ _____ is an accounting period that runs for any 12 consecutive months.

2. _____ _____ are prepared for parts of a fiscal year (monthly, quarterly, etc.).

3. The _____ _____ _____ eliminates the need for footings.

4. The positive balance of each account is referred to as its _____ _____ .

5. The process of recording transactions in a journal is called _____ .

6. Entries are journalized in _____ _____ .

7. A ledger is often called a _____ _____ _____ _____ .

8. The _____ portion of a journal entry is indented and placed below the _____ portion.

9. A journal entry requiring three or more accounts is called a _____ _____ _____ .

10. Prepaid rent is a(n) _____ on the balance sheet.

11. When supplies are used up or consumed they become a(n) _____ .

12. The book of original entry usually refers to a(n) _____ .

13. The process of transferring information from a journal to a ledger is called _____ .

14. _____ deals with the process of updating the PR of the journal from the account number of the ledger to indicate to which account in the ledger information has been posted.

15. Recording $885.000 as $88.50 is an example of a _____ .

Part II Instructions

Match the term in column A to the definition, example, or phrase in column B. Be sure to use a letter only once.

COLUMN A

____g____ **1.** EXAMPLE: Book of original entry

_____ **2.** Withdrawals

_____ **3.** Slide

_____ **4.** Transposition

_____ **5.** Posting

_____ **6.** General Journal

_____ **7.** Cross-reference

_____ **8.** Journalizing

_____ **9.** Balance Sheet prepared monthly

_____ **10.** A fiscal year

COLUMN B

a. 118 — 1180

b. Transferring information from a general journal to a ledger

c. Chronological order

d. Increased by a credit

e. Non-business expense

f. Compound journal entry

g. General journal

h. Rearrangement of digits of a number by accident

i. Updating PR column of journal from ledger account

j. Trial balance

k. Place to record transactions

l. Accounting cycle

m. Accounting period

n. Interim statements

Part III Instructions

Answer true or false to the following statements.

1. 5,187 written by mistake as 5,178 is an example of a slide.
2. The totals of a trial balance may possibly not balance due to transpositions.
3. Withdrawals has a normal balance of a credit.
4. The running balance of an account can be kept in a four-column account.
5. The journal links debits and credits in alphabetical order.
6. The ledger accumulates information from the journal.
7. The post reference column of a ledger records the account number of that account.
8. An accounting cycle must be from January 1 to December 31.
9. The ledger is the book of original entry.
10. The income statement is prepared for a specific accounting period.
11. Interim statements are prepared for an entire fiscal year.
12. A calendar year could be a fiscal year.
13. 150 written by mistake as 1,500 is an example of a slide.

14. If the totals of a trial balance balance, the individual balance of items must be correct.

15. The equality of debits and credits on a trial balance does not guarantee that transactions have been properly recorded.

16. The trial balance is prepared from the journal.

17. Cross-referencing means never updating the post reference column of the journal.

18. Journals and ledgers are always in the same book.

19. The normal balance of each account is located on the same side that increases the acccount.

20. Ruling of four-column accounts is eliminated.

CHAPTER 3
SOLUTIONS TO SUMMARY PRACTICE TEST

Part I

1. fiscal year
2. interim statements
3. four-column ledger
4. normal balance
5. journalizing
6. chronological order
7. book of final entry
8. credit, debit
9. compound journal entry
10. asset
11. expense
12. journal
13. posting
14. cross-reference
15. slide

Part II

1. g
2. e
3. a
4. h
5. b
6. k
7. i
8. c
9. n
10. m

Part III

1. false
2. true
3. false
4. true
5. false
6. true
7. false
8. false
9. false
10. true
11. false
12. true
13. true
14. false
15. true
16. false
17. false
18. false
19. true
20. true

CONTINUING PROBLEM FOR CHAPTER 3

SANCHEZ COMPUTER CENTER
GENERAL JOURNAL

PAGE 1

Date	Account Titles and Description	PR	Dr.	Cr.

SANCHEZ COMPUTER CENTER
GENERAL JOURNAL

Date	Account Titles and Description	PR	Dr.	Cr.

CASH   **ACCOUNT NO. 1000**

Date		Explanation	Post Ref.	Debit	Credit	Balance Debit	Balance Credit
9/1	0X	Balance forward	✔			2 8 6 5 00	

ACCOUNTS RECEIVABLE   ACCOUNT NO. 1020

Date		Explanation	Post Ref.	Debit	Credit	Balance	
						Debit	Credit
9/1	0X	Balance forward	✔			8 5 0 00	

PREPAID RENT   ACCOUNT NO. 1025

Date	Explanation	Post Ref.	Debit	Credit	Balance	
					Debit	Credit

SUPPLIES   ACCOUNT NO. 1030

Date		Explanation	Post Ref.	Debit	Credit	Balance	
						Debit	Credit
9/1	0X	Balance forward	✔			4 5 0 00	

COMPUTER SHOP EQUIPMENT   ACCOUNT NO. 1080

Date		Explanation	Post Ref.	Debit	Credit	Balance	
						Debit	Credit
9/1	0X		✔			1 2 0 0 00	

OFFICE EQUIPMENT   ACCOUNT NO. 1090

Date		Explanation	Post Ref.	Debit	Credit	Balance Debit	Balance Credit
9/1	0X	Balance forward	✔			6 0 0 00	

ACCOUNTS PAYABLE   ACCOUNT NO. 2000

Date		Explanation	Post Ref.	Debit	Credit	Balance Debit	Balance Credit
9/1	0X	Balance forward	✔				4 0 5 00

FREEDMAN, CAPITAL   ACCOUNT NO. 3000

Date		Explanation	Post Ref.	Debit	Credit	Balance Debit	Balance Credit
9/1	0X	Balance forward	✔				4 5 0 0 00

FREEDMAN, WITHDRAWALS   ACCOUNT NO. 3010

Date		Explanation	Post Ref.	Debit	Credit	Balance Debit	Balance Credit
9/1	0X	Balance forward	✔			1 0 0 00	

SERVICE REVENUE   ACCOUNT NO. <u>4000</u>

Date		Explanation	Post Ref.	Debit	Credit	Balance Debit	Balance Credit
9/1	0X	Balance forward	✓				3 4 0 0 00

ADVERTISING EXPENSE   ACCOUNT NO. <u>5010</u>

Date		Explanation	Post Ref.	Debit	Credit	Balance Debit	Balance Credit
9/1	0X	Balance forward	✓			1 4 0 0 00	

RENT EXPENSE   ACCOUNT NO. <u>5020</u>

Date		Explanation	Post Ref.	Debit	Credit	Balance Debit	Balance Credit
9/1	0X	Balance forward	✓			4 0 0 00	

UTILITIES EXPENSE   ACCOUNT NO. 5030

Date		Explanation	Post Ref.	Debit	Credit	Balance Debit	Balance Credit
9/1	0X	Balance forward	✔			8 5 00	

PHONE EXPENSE   ACCOUNT NO. 5040

Date		Explanation	Post Ref.	Debit	Credit	Balance Debit	Balance Credit
9/1	0X	Balance forward	✔			1 5 5 00	

SUPPLIES EXPENSE   ACCOUNT NO. 5050

Date	Explanation	Post Ref.	Debit	Credit	Balance Debit	Balance Credit

INSURANCE EXPENSE   ACCOUNT NO. 5060

Date		Explanation	Post Ref.	Debit	Credit	Balance	
						Debit	Credit
9/1	0X	Balance forward	✔			1 5 0 00	

POSTAGE EXPENSE   ACCOUNT NO. 5070

Date		Explanation	Post Ref.	Debit	Credit	Balance	
						Debit	Credit
9/1	0X	Balance forward	✔			5 0 00	

SANCHEZ COMPUTER CENTER
TRIAL BALANCE
SEPTEMBER 30, 200X

		Dr.	Cr.

SANCHEZ COMPUTER CENTER
INCOME STATEMENT
FOR THE QUARTER ENDED 9/30/0X

SANCHEZ COMPUTER CENTER
STATEMENT OF OWNER'S EQUITY
FOR THE QUARTER ENDED 9/30/0X

Name _____ Class _____ Date _____

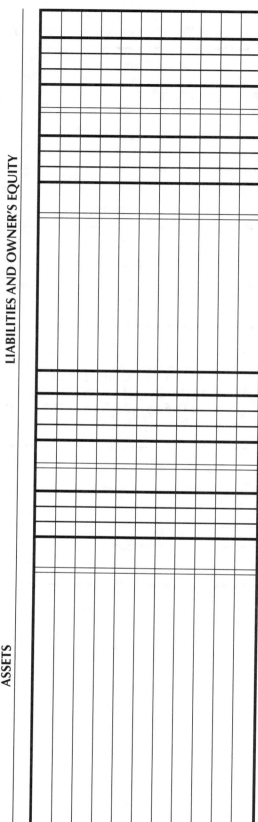

SANCHEZ COMPUTER CENTER
BALANCE SHEET
9/30/OX

ASSETS

LIABILITIES AND OWNER'S EQUITY

ACCOUNTING CYCLE CONTINUED: PREPARING WORKSHEETS AND FINANCIAL STATEMENTS

4

SELF-REVIEW QUIZ 4-1

Use a blank fold-out worksheet located at the end of this text.

SELF-REVIEW QUIZ 4-2

(1) _____

_____

_____

(2) _____

_____

_____

(3)

ASSETS

LIABILITIES AND OWNER'S EQUITY

FORMS FOR DEMONSTRATION PROBLEM

(1)

Use a blank fold-out worksheet located at the end of this text.

(2)

FROST COMPANY
INCOME STATEMENT
FOR MONTH ENDED DECEMBER 31, 200X

(2)

FROST COMPANY
STATEMENT OF OWNER'S EQUITY
FOR MONTH ENDED DECEMBER 31, 200X

DEMONSTRATION PROBLEM (CONCLUDED)

(2)

FROST COMPANY
BALANCE SHEET
DECEMBER 31, 200X

ASSETS

LIABILITIES AND OWNER'S EQUITY

CHAPTER 4
FORMS FOR CLASSROOM DEMONSTRATION EXERCISES SET A OR SET B

1. A. _____
    _____
    _____

    B.

1 Accounts Affected	2 Category	3 ↑ ↓	4 Rules	5 T-Account

    C. _____
    _____
    _____
    _____

2. A. _____
    _____
    _____

    B.

1 Accounts Affected	2 Category	3 ↑ ↓	4 Rules	5 T-Account

    C. _____

3. A. _____
    B. _____
    C.

1 Accounts Affected	2 Category	3 ↑ ↓	4 Rules	5 T-Account

    D. _____
    _____
    _____

4. A.

1 Accounts Affected	2 Category	3 ↑ ↓	4 Rules	5 T-Account

B. _____
_____
_____

5.

A. _____   H. _____
B. _____   I. _____
C. _____   J. _____
D. _____   K. _____
E. _____   L. _____
F. _____   M. _____
G. _____   N. _____

6.

_____
_____
_____
_____
_____
_____
_____
_____
_____
_____

FORMS FOR EXERCISES

4.1.

Account	Category	Normal Balance	Financial Statement(s) Found on

4-2.

Accounts Affected	Category	↑ ↓	Rules	Amount
A.				
B.				

4-3.

A. _____

B. _____

_____

4-4.

Use a blank fold-out worksheet located at the end of this text.

EXERCISES (CONTINUED)

4-5.

(A)

J. TRENT
INCOME STATEMENT
FOR MONTH ENDED DECEMBER 31, 200X

(B)

J. TRENT
STATEMENT OF OWNER'S EQUITY
FOR MONTH ENDED DECEMBER 31, 200X

EXERCISES (CONTINUED)
(C)

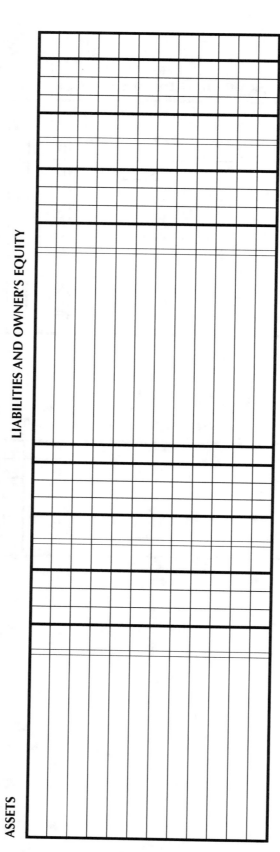

J. TRENT
BALANCE SHEET
DECEMBER 31, 200X

ASSETS

LIABILITIES AND OWNER'S EQUITY

END OF CHAPTER PROBLEMS

PROBLEM 4A-1 OR PROBLEM 4B-1

Use a blank fold-out worksheet located at the end of this text.

PROBLEM 4A-2 OR PROBLEM 4B-2

Use a blank fold-out worksheet located at the end of this text.

PROBLEM 4A-3 OR PROBLEM 4B-3

Use a blank fold-out worksheet located at the end of this text.

(2)

KEVIN'S MOVING CO.
INCOME STATEMENT
FOR MONTH ENDED OCTOBER 31, 200X

KEVIN'S MOVING CO.
STATEMENT OF OWNER'S EQUITY
FOR MONTH ENDED OCTOBER 31, 200X

(2)

PROBLEM 4A-3 OR PROBLEM 4B-3

(2)

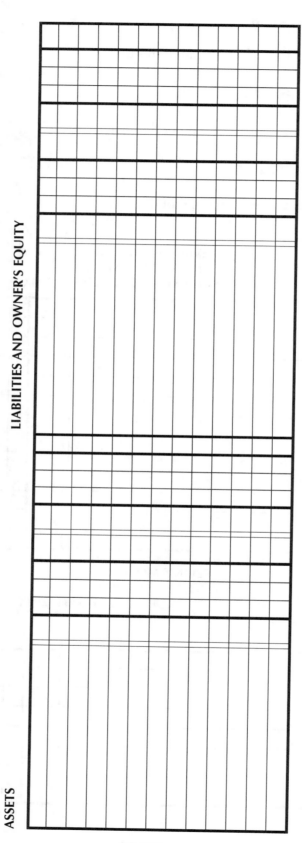

KEVIN'S MOVING CO.
BALANCE SHEET
OCTOBER 31, 200X

LIABILITIES AND OWNER'S EQUITY

ASSETS

PROBLEM 4A-4 OR PROBLEM 4B-4

Use a blank fold-out worksheet located at the end of this text.

(2)

DICK'S REPAIR SERVICE
INCOME STATEMENT
FOR MONTH ENDED NOVEMBER 30, 200X

(2)

DICK'S REPAIR SERVICE
STATEMENT OF OWNER'S EQUITY
FOR MONTH ENDED NOVEMBER 30, 200X

PROBLEM 4A-4 OR PROBLEM 4B-4 (CONCLUDED)

(2)

DICK'S REPAIR SERVICE
BALANCE SHEET
NOVEMBER 30, 200X

ASSETS

LIABILITIES AND OWNER'S EQUITY

CHAPTER 4
SUMMARY PRACTICE TEST:
THE ACCOUNTING CYCLE CONTINUED:
PREPARING WORKSHEETS AND FINANCIAL STATEMENTS

Part I Instructions

Fill in the blank(s) to complete the statement.

1. Adjustments are the result of _____ transactions.
2. A _____ will increase accumulated depreciation.
3. _____ affect both the income statement and balance sheet.
4. The adjustment for supplies reflects the amount of supplies _____.
5. Supplies Expense is found on the income statement. Supplies are found on

   _____ _____.
6. _____ _____ reflects the cost of equipment at time of purchase.
7. Depreciation Expense is found on the _____ _____.
8. _____ _____ is a contra asset that has a credit balance.
9. Accumulated Depreciation, a contra asset, is found on the _____ _____.
10. Historical or original cost of an auto less _____

    _____ reflects the unused amount of the auto on the accounting books.
11. Withdrawals are found in the _____ column of the balance sheet section of the worksheet.
12. Salaries Payable is a liability that will appear in the _____

    _____ _____ _____ of the worksheet.
13. The figure for net income on the worksheet is carried over to the _____ column of the balance sheet.
14. A worksheet is a(n) _____ report.
15. _____ _____ are prepared after the

    completion of the worksheet.

Part II Instructions

Complete the following statements by circling the letter of the appropriate answer.

1. Adjustments will affect
   a. the balance sheet
   b. the income statement
   c. both a and b
2. The historical or original cost of an asset on the worksheet
   a. never changes
   b. sometimes changes
   c. continually changes
3. Net income on the worksheet is
   a. carried over to the trial balance
   b. carried over to the adjusted trial balance
   c. carried over to the balance sheet column
4. Accumulated Depreciation is found on
   a. a worksheet
   b. an income statement
   c. both a worksheet and an income statement
5. Accumulated Depreciation, a contra asset, is increased by a
   a. debit
   b. credit
   c. both a and b
6. A worksheet is usually competed
   a. one column at a time
   b. two columns at a time
   c. three columns at a time
7. Withdrawals on the worksheet are found in the
   a. debit column of the income statement
   b. debit column of the balance sheet
   c. both a and b
8. The worksheet specifically shows the
   a. beginning figure for owner capital
   b. ending figure for owner capital
   c. average figure for owner capital
9. The total of the assets on a formal balance sheet will _____ equal the total of the debit column of the balance sheet on the worksheet.
   a. always
   b. sometimes
   c. never
10. The adjustment for depreciation affects
    a. the income statement
    b. the balance sheet
    c. both a and b
11. The adjustment for supplies requires one to know
    a. beginning supplies plus supplies purchased
    b. supplies on hand
    c. both a and b

12. The purpose of adjustments is to
    a. bring general journals up to date
    b. bring ledger accounts up to proper balances in the journal
    c. bring ledger accounts to proper balance
13. Book values equals cost less
    a. expenses
    b. accumulated depreciation
    c. neither a nor b
14. The _____ is an informal report.
    a. income statement
    b. balance sheet
    c. worksheet

Part III Instructions

Answer true or false to the following statements.

1. The normal balance of accumulated depreciation is a debit.
2. Assets are only income statement accounts.
3. The total of the adjustments column may balance but be incorrect.
4. Prepaid rent is found on the income statement.
5. Rent expense is found on the income statement.
6. Debits and credits are found on financial statements.
7. Historical cost relates only to automobiles.
8. Accumulated Depreciation is found on the income statement.
9. As Accumulated Depreciation increases, the historical cost changes.
10. The adjustment for depreciation directly affects cash.
11. An expense is only recorded when it is paid.
12. The ending figure for owner capital does not have to be calculated from the worksheet.
13. Withdrawals have the same balance as Accumulated Depreciation.
14. Salaries Payable is an asset on the income statement.
15. Net loss would never be shown on a worksheet.
16. The net income on the worksheet is the same amount on the income statement.
17. Worksheets must use dollar signs.
18. The worksheet eliminates the need to prepare financial statements.
19. Cost less accumulated depreciation equals book value.
20. Accrued Salaries are expenses that have already been paid for.

CHAPTER 4
SOLUTIONS TO SUMMARY PRACTICE TEST

Part I

1. internal
2. credit
3. adjustments
4. used up
5. balance sheet
6. historical (original) cost
7. income statement
8. Accumulated Depreciation
9. balance sheet
10. accumulated depreciation
11. debit
12. balance sheet credit column
13. credit
14. informal
15. financial statements

Part II

1. c
2. a
3. c
4. a
5. b
6. b
7. b
8. a
9. c
10. c
11. c
12. c
13. b
14. c

Part III

1. false
2. false
3. true
4. false
5. true
6. false
7. false
8. false
9. false
10. false
11. false
12. true
13. false
14. false
15. false
16. true
17. false
18. false
19. true
20. false

CONTINUING PROBLEM FOR CHAPTER 4*

SANCHEZ COMPUTER CENTER
INCOME STATEMENT
FOR THE THREE MONTHS ENDED SEPTEMBER 30, 200X

SANCHEZ COMPUTER CENTER
STATEMENT OF OWNER'S EQUITY
FOR THE THREE MONTHS ENDED SEPTEMBER 30, 200X

*Use a blank fold-out worksheet located at the end of this text.

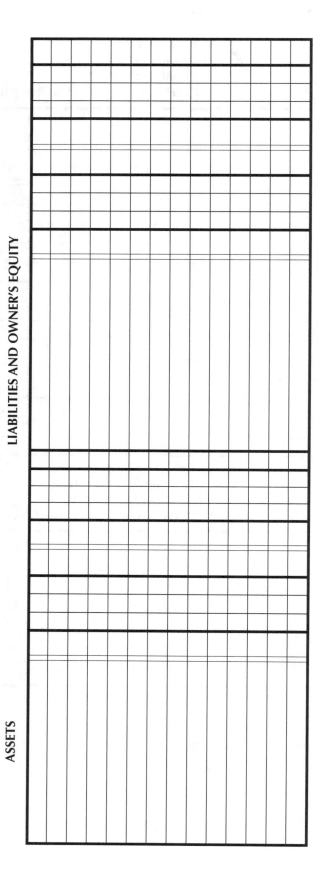

SANCHEZ COMPUTER CENTER
BALANCE SHEET
SEPTEMBER 30, 200X

ASSETS

LIABILITIES AND OWNER'S EQUITY

THE ACCOUNTING CYCLE COMPLETED: ADJUSTING, CLOSING, AND THE POST-CLOSING TRIAL BALANCE

SELF-REVIEW QUIZ 5-1

(1)

Date	Account Titles and Description	PR	Dr.	Cr.

(2) Partial Ledger

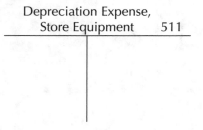

Depreciation Expense,
Store Equipment   511

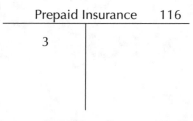

Prepaid Insurance   116

3

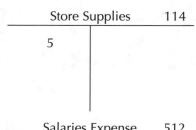

Store Supplies   114

5

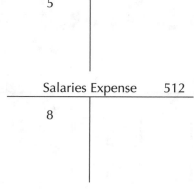

Salaries Expense   512

8

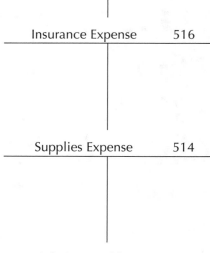

Accumulated Depreciation,
Store Equipment   122

4

Insurance Expense   516

Supplies Expense   514

Salaries Payable   212

SELF-REVIEW QUIZ 5-2

P. Logan, Capital 310	Revenue from Clients 410	Supplies Expense 514
14	25	4

P. Logan, Withdrawals 311	Depreciation Expense, Store Equipment 510	Insurance Expense 516
3	1	2

Income Summary 312	Salaries Expense 512	Rent Expense 518
	11	2

(2) _____

_____

_____

_____

SELF-REVIEW QUIZ 5-3

_____

_____

_____

FORMS FOR DEMONSTRATION PROBLEM

(Worksheet is a fold-out at end of text)

ROLO COMPANY
GENERAL JOURNAL

PAGE 1

Date	Account Titles and Description	PR	Dr.	Cr.

FORMS FOR DEMONSTRATION PROBLEM (CONTINUED)

ROLO COMPANY
GENERAL JOURNAL

PAGE 2

Date	Account Titles and Description	PR	Dr.	Cr.

FORMS FOR DEMONSTRATION PROBLEM (CONTINUED)

CASH   ACCOUNT NO. 111

Date	Explanation	Post Ref.	Debit	Credit	Balance Debit	Balance Credit

ACCOUNTS RECEIVABLE   ACCOUNT NO. 112

Date	Explanation	Post Ref.	Debit	Credit	Balance Debit	Balance Credit

PREPAID RENT   ACCOUNT NO. 114

Date	Explanation	Post Ref.	Debit	Credit	Balance Debit	Balance Credit

OFFICE SUPPLIES   ACCOUNT NO. 115

Date	Explanation	Post Ref.	Debit	Credit	Balance Debit	Balance Credit

FORMS FOR DEMONSTRATION PROBLEM (CONTINUED)

OFFICE EQUIPMENT   **ACCOUNT NO. 121**

Date	Explanation	Post Ref.	Debit	Credit	Balance Debit	Balance Credit

ACCUMULATED DEPRECIATION, OFFICE EQUIPMENT   ACCOUNT NO. 122

Date	Explanation	Post Ref.	Debit	Credit	Balance Debit	Balance Credit

ACCOUNTS PAYABLE   **ACCOUNT NO. 211**

Date	Explanation	Post Ref.	Debit	Credit	Balance Debit	Balance Credit

FORMS FOR DEMONSTRATION PROBLEM (CONTINUED)

SALARIES PAYABLE   ACCOUNT NO. <u>212</u>

Date		Explanation	Post Ref.	Debit	Credit	Balance	
						Debit	Credit

ROLO KERN, CAPITAL   ACCOUNT NO. <u>311</u>

Date		Explanation	Post Ref.	Debit	Credit	Balance	
						Debit	Credit

ROLO KERN, WITHDRAWALS   ACCOUNT NO. <u>312</u>

Date		Explanation	Post Ref.	Debit	Credit	Balance	
						Debit	Credit

INCOME SUMMARY   ACCOUNT NO. <u>313</u>

Date		Explanation	Post Ref.	Debit	Credit	Balance	
						Debit	Credit

FEES EARNED   ACCOUNT NO. <u>411</u>

Date		Explanation	Post Ref.	Debit	Credit	Balance	
						Debit	Credit

FORMS FOR DEMONSTRATION PROBLEM (CONTINUED)

SALARIES EXPENSE   ACCOUNT NO. 511

Date		Explanation	Post Ref.	Debit	Credit	Balance	
						Debit	Credit

ADVERTISING EXPENSE   ACCOUNT NO. 512

Date		Explanation	Post Ref.	Debit	Credit	Balance	
						Debit	Credit

RENT EXPENSE   ACCOUNT NO. 513

Date		Explanation	Post Ref.	Debit	Credit	Balance	
						Debit	Credit

OFFICE SUPPLIES EXPENSE   ACCOUNT NO. 514

Date		Explanation	Post Ref.	Debit	Credit	Balance	
						Debit	Credit

DEPRECIATION EXPENSE, OFFICE EQUIPMENT   ACCOUNT NO. 515

Date		Explanation	Post Ref.	Debit	Credit	Balance	
						Debit	Credit

FORMS FOR DEMONSTRATION PROBLEM (CONTINUED)

ROLO COMPANY
INCOME STATEMENT
FOR MONTH ENDED JANUARY 31, 200X

ROLO COMPANY
STATEMENT OF OWNER'S EQUITY
FOR MONTH ENDED JANUARY 31, 200X

FORMS FOR DEMONSTRATION PROBLEM (CONCLUDED)

ROLO COMPANY
BALANCE SHEET
JANUARY 31, 200X

ASSETS

LIABILITIES AND OWNER'S EQUITY

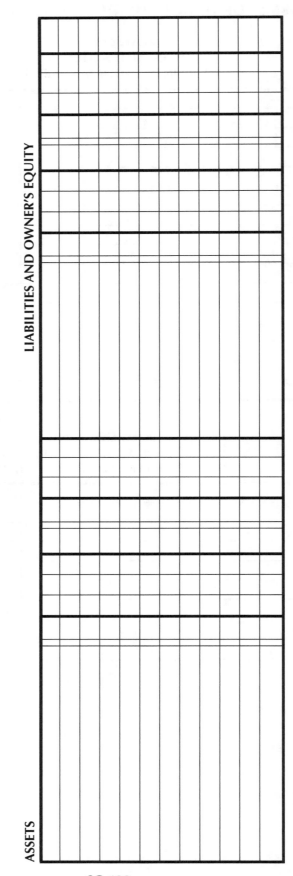

FORMS FOR DEMONSTRATION PROBLEM (CONCLUDED)

ROLO COMPANY
POST-CLOSING TRIAL BALANCE
JANUARY 31, 200X

		Dr.		Cr.	

CHAPTER 5
FORMS FOR DEMONSTRATION CLASSROOM EXERCISES SET A OR SET B

GENERAL JOURNAL

1.

PAGE 3

Date	Account Titles and Description	PR	Dr.	Cr.

Prepaid Insurance 115	Insurance Expense 510
Store Supplies 116	Depreciation Expense, Store Equipment 512
Accumulated Depreciation Store Equipment 119	Supplies Expense 514
Salaries Payable 210	Salaries Expense 516

2. _____
_____
_____
_____
_____
_____
_____
_____
_____

3.

4.

Income Summary   314

_____

5.

Mel Blanc, Capital   310

_____

FORMS FOR EXERCISES

5-1.

Date	Account Titles and Description	PR	Dr.	Cr.

5-2.

TEMPORARY	PERMANENT	WILL BE CLOSED
_____	_____	_____

1. Income Summary
2. Jen Rich, Capital
3. Salary Expense
4. Jen Rich, Withdrawals
5. Fees Earned
6. Accounts Payable
7. Cash

5-3.

Date		Account Titles and Description	PR		Dr.	Cr.

EXERCISES (CONTINUED)

5-4.

Date		Account Titles and Description	PR		Dr.			Cr.		

5-5.

WEY CO.
POST-CLOSING TRIAL BALANCE
DECEMBER 31, 200X

		Dr.			Cr.		

Name _____ Class _____ Date _____

PROBLEM 5A-1 OR PROBLEM 5B-1

Use a blank fold-out worksheet located at the end of this text.

(2)

MEL'S ACCOUNTING SERVICE
GENERAL JOURNAL

Date	Account Titles and Description	PR	Dr.	Cr.
	Insurance Expense		2 00	
	Pre Paid Insurance			2 00 ✓
	Deprec. Expense Equip.		2 00	
	Accum. Deprec. Equip.			2 00 ✓
	Supplie Expense		9 00	
	Supplies			9 00 ✓
	Salaries Expense		3 00 ✓	
	Salaries Payable			3 00 ✓
	Post closing Trial Balance			
	Cash		30 000 ✓	
	Acct. Receivable		6 500	
	Prepaid Insurance		2 00	
	Supplies		6 00	
	Equipment		3 000	
	Accm Deprec. Equipment			2 1 00 ✓
	Acct Payable			11 0 0 0 ✓
	Salaries Payable			3 00 ✓
	Mel. Franks Capital			26 9 00 ✓
			40 3 00 ✓	40 3 00 ✓

Name _____ Class _____ Date _____

PROBLEM 5A-2 OR PROBLEM 5B-2

(1)

POTTER CLEANING SERVICE
GENERAL JOURNAL

Date	Account Titles and Description	PR	Dr.	Cr.
	Insurance Expense		180 —	
	Prepaid Insurance			180 —
	Cleaning Supplies Expense		100	
	Cleaning Supplies			100 —
	Depr. Expense Auto		150 —	
	Accum. Depr. Auto			150 —
	Salaries Expense		160	
	Salaries Payable		300 —	160 —
				300
	Cleaning Fees		4 680 —	
	Income Summary			4 680 —
	Income Summary		2 650	2 650
	Salarie Expense		1 600 —	1 600 —
	Telephone Expense		264 —	264 —
	Advertising Expense		196	196 —
	Gas Expense		160	160 —
	Insurance Expense		180	180 —
	Cleaning Supplies Exp.		100	100 —
	Depr. Expense		150	150 —
	Income Summary		540	
	B. Potter Capital			540 —
	B. Potter Capital		460	
	B. Potter Withdrawals			460 —

SG-136

PROBLEM 5A-2 OR PROBLEM 5B-2 (CONTINUED)

CASH — ACCOUNT NO. 112

Date	Explanation	Post Ref.	Debit	Credit	Balance Debit	Balance Credit
	Cash		400 -		400 -	

PREPAID INSURANCE — ACCOUNT NO. 114

Date	Explanation	Post Ref.	Debit	Credit	Balance Debit	Balance Credit
			520 -		520	
				180	340 -	

CLEANING SUPPLIES — ACCOUNT NO. 115

Date	Explanation	Post Ref.	Debit	Credit	Balance Debit	Balance Credit
			144 -		144	
				100	44 -	

AUTO — ACCOUNT NO. 121

Date	Explanation	Post Ref.	Debit	Credit	Balance Debit	Balance Credit
			2720 -		2720 -	
					2720 -	

ACCUMULATED DEPRECIATION, AUTO — ACCOUNT NO. 122

Date	Explanation	Post Ref.	Debit	Credit	Balance Debit	Balance Credit
				860 -		860 -
				150		1010 -

PROBLEM 5A-2 OR PROBLEM 5B-2 (CONTINUED)

ACCOUNTS PAYABLE   ACCOUNT NO. 212

Date	Explanation	Post Ref.	Debit	Credit	Balance Debit	Balance Credit
				224		224

SALARIES PAYABLE   ACCOUNT NO. 213

Date	Explanation	Post Ref.	Debit	Credit	Balance Debit	Balance Credit
				160		160

B. POTTER, CAPITAL   ACCOUNT NO. 312

Date	Explanation	Post Ref.	Debit	Credit	Balance Debit	Balance Credit
				540		540

B. POTTER, WITHDRAWALS   ACCOUNT NO. 313

Date	Explanation	Post Ref.	Debit	Credit	Balance Debit	Balance Credit
			460		460	

INCOME SUMMARY   ACCOUNT NO. 314

Date	Explanation	Post Ref.	Debit	Credit	Balance Debit	Balance Credit
	Closing Revenue			4680	4680	2460
	Closing Expense		2460		2030	
	Closing Net Income		2030			2030

PROBLEM 5A-2 OR PROBLEM 5B-2 (CONTINUED)

CLEANING FEES   ACCOUNT NO. 412

Date		Explanation	Post Ref.	Debit	Credit	Balance Debit	Balance Credit
					4 6 8 0 —	4 6 8 0 —	4 6 8 0 —
							4 6 8 0 —

SALARIES EXPENSE   ACCOUNT NO. 513

Date		Explanation	Post Ref.	Debit	Credit	Balance Debit	Balance Credit
				1 4 4 0 —		1 4 4 0 —	
				1 6 0		1 6 0 0	

TELEPHONE EXPENSE   ACCOUNT NO. 514

Date		Explanation	Post Ref.	Debit	Credit	Balance Debit	Balance Credit
				2 6 4 —		2 6 4 —	

ADVERTISING EXPENSE   ACCOUNT NO. 515

Date		Explanation	Post Ref.	Debit	Credit	Balance Debit	Balance Credit
				1 9 6 —		1 9 6 —	

GAS EXPENSE   ACCOUNT NO. 516

Date		Explanation	Post Ref.	Debit	Credit	Balance Debit	Balance Credit
				1 6 0 —		1 6 0 —	

PROBLEM 5A-2 OR PROBLEM 5B-2 (CONTINUED)

INSURANCE EXPENSE   ACCOUNT NO. 517

Date	Explanation	Post Ref.	Debit	Credit	Balance	
					Debit	Credit
			1 8 0 —		1 8 0 —	

CLEANING SUPPLIES EXPENSE   ACCOUNT NO. 518

Date	Explanation	Post Ref.	Debit	Credit	Balance	
					Debit	Credit
			1 0 0 —		1 0 0 —	

DEPRECIATION EXPENSE, AUTO   ACCOUNT NO. 519

Date	Explanation	Post Ref.	Debit	Credit	Balance	
					Debit	Credit
			1 5 0 —		1 5 0 —	

PROBLEM 5A-2 OR PROBLEM 5B-2 (CONCLUDED)

POTTER CLEANING SERVICE
POST-CLOSING TRIAL BALANCE
MARCH 31, 200X

	Dr.	Cr.
Cash	400 —	
Prepaid Insurance	340 —	
Cleaning Supplies	44	
Auto	2720 —	
Accm. Depr. Auto		1000 —
Acct Payable		224 —
Salaries Payable		160 —
B. Potter, Capital		2110 —
Totals	3504	3504

PROBLEM 5A-3 OR PROBLEM 5B-3

Use a blank fold-out worksheet located at the end of this text.

PROBLEM 5A-3 OR PROBLEM 5B-3 (CONTINUED)

PETE'S PLOWING
GENERAL JOURNAL

PAGE 1

Date	Account Titles and Description	PR	Dr.	Cr.
Jan 1	Cash	111	7000 —	
	Pete, Capital	311		7000 —
1	Equipment	123	6000	
	Pete Capital	311		6000 —
1	Prepaid Rent	114	2000	
	Cash	111		2000 —
4	Office Equipment	121	7200	
	Acct. Payable			7200 —
6	Snow Supplies	115	700	
	Cash	111		700 —
8	Cash	111	15000	
	Snow Plowing Fees Earned	411		15000 —
12				
	Pete Mack Withdrawals	312	1000 —	
	Cash	111		1000 —
20	Snow Supplies Expense	112	5000 —	
	Snow Plowing Fees Earned	411		5000 —
26	Salary Expense	511	1800	
	Cash	111		1800 —
28	Acct Payable	211	3600	
	Cash	111		3600 —
29	Advertising Expense	512	900	
	Acct Payable	211		900

PROBLEM 5A-3 OR PROBLEM 5B-3 (CONTINUED)

PETE'S PLOWING
GENERAL JOURNAL

PAGE 2

Date	Account Titles and Description	PR	Dr.	Cr.
30	Telephone Expense	513	2 1 0 -	
	Cash	111		2 1 0 -
	Supplies Expense		3 0 0	
	Snow Supplies			3 0 0 -
	Rent Expense		6 0 0	
	Prepaid Rent			6 0 0 -
	Deprec. expense office equipment	516	1 2 0	
	Accm. Depr. office equipment			1 2 0 -
	Depr. expense snow equipment		1 0 0	
	Accum Depr. Equipment			1 0 0 -
	Salarie Expense		1 9 0	
	Salaries Payable			1 9 0 -

PROBLEM 5A-3 OR PROBLEM 5B-3 (CONTINUED)

PETE'S PLOWING
GENERAL JOURNAL

PAGE 3

Date	Account Titles and Description	PR	Dr.	Cr.
	Cash		12 6 9 0 —	
	Acct Rec.		5 0 0 0	
	Pre Paid Rent		1 4 0 0	
	Snow Supplies		4 0 0	
	Office Equipment		7 2 0 0	
	Accm. Depr. Office Equipment			1 2 0 —
	Snow Equipment		6 0 0 0	
	Accm. Depr. Snow Equipment			1 0 0 —
	Acct Payable			4 5 0 0 —
	Salaries Payable			1 9 0 —
	Pete Mack, Capital		13 0 0 0 —	13 0 0 0 —
	Pete Mack, Withdrawals		1 0 0 0	
	Plowing Fees			20 0 0 0 —
	Salaries Expense		1 9 9 0	
	Advertising Expense		9 0 0	
	Rent Expense		6 0 0	
	Snow Supplies Expense		5 3 0 0	
	Depr Expense Equipment Office		1 2 0	
	Depr Expense Equipment Snow		1 0 0	
	Telephone Expense		2 1 0	
			37 9 1 0	37 9 1 0 —

PROBLEM 5A-3 OR PROBLEM 5B-3 (CONTINUED)

CASH   ACCOUNT NO. 111

Date		Explanation	Post Ref.	Debit	Credit	Balance Debit	Balance Credit
		Invested		7000		7000	
		Rent			2000	5000	
		Supplies			700	4300	
		Fees Earned		15000		19300	
		Withdrawal Personal uses			1000	18300	
		Salaries Paid			1800	16500	
		Paid for Equipment			3600	12900	
		Paid Telephone Bill			210	12690	

ACCOUNTS RECEIVABLE   ACCOUNT NO. 112

Date		Explanation	Post Ref.	Debit	Credit	Balance Debit	Balance Credit
		Fees Earned		5000 —		5000 —	
		Telephone Bill		900		5900	

PREPAID RENT   ACCOUNT NO. 114

Date		Explanation	Post Ref.	Debit	Credit	Balance Debit	Balance Credit
		rent for 3 months		2000 —			
		Rent used			600	1400 —	

SNOW SUPPLIES   ACCOUNT NO. 115

Date		Explanation	Post Ref.	Debit	Credit	Balance Debit	Balance Credit
				700		700 —	
		Used			300	400	

Name _____ Class _____ Date _____

PROBLEM 5A-3 OR PROBLEM 5B-3 (CONTINUED)

OFFICE EQUIPMENT   ACCOUNT NO. 121

Date	Explanation	Post Ref.	Debit	Credit	Balance Debit	Balance Credit
	Purchase Equip.		7200		7200 —	

ACCUMULATED DEPRECIATION, OFFICE EQUIPMENT   ACCOUNT NO. 122

Date	Explanation	Post Ref.	Debit	Credit	Balance Debit	Balance Credit
				120		120

SNOW EQUIPMENT   ACCOUNT NO. 123

Date	Explanation	Post Ref.	Debit	Credit	Balance Debit	Balance Credit
	Investment		6000		6000 —	

ACCUMULATED DEPRECIATION, SNOW EQUIPMENT   ACCOUNT NO. 124

Date	Explanation	Post Ref.	Debit	Credit	Balance Debit	Balance Credit
				100		100

ACCOUNTS PAYABLE   ACCOUNT NO. 211

Date	Explanation	Post Ref.	Debit	Credit	Balance Debit	Balance Credit
	Equipment			7200 —	7200	7200 —
	owned Equipment		3600			3600 —
	Advertising Bill			900		4500 —

SG-146

PROBLEM 5A-3 OR PROBLEM 5B-3 (CONTINUED)

SALARIES PAYABLE   ACCOUNT NO. 212

Date	Explanation	Post Ref.	Debit	Credit	Balance Debit	Balance Credit
				1 9 0 —		

PETE MACK, CAPITAL   ACCOUNT NO. 311

Date	Explanation	Post Ref.	Debit	Credit	Balance Debit	Balance Credit
	investment		13 000 —			

PETE MACK, WITHDRAWALS   ACCOUNT NO. 312

Date	Explanation	Post Ref.	Debit	Credit	Balance Debit	Balance Credit
	Personal Uses		1 000 —		1 000 —	

INCOME SUMMARY   ACCOUNT NO. 313

Date	Explanation	Post Ref.	Debit	Credit	Balance Debit	Balance Credit

PLOWING FEES   ACCOUNT NO. 411

Date	Explanation	Post Ref.	Debit	Credit	Balance Debit	Balance Credit
	Plowing Shopping Center			15 000 —		15 000 —
	" " North East Co			5 000		20 000 —

PROBLEM 5A-3 OR PROBLEM 5B-3 (CONTINUED)

SALARIES EXPENSE — ACCOUNT NO. 511

Date	Explanation	Post Ref.	Debit	Credit	Balance Debit	Balance Credit
	Salaries Paid		1800 —		1800 —	
			190		1990 —	

ADVERTISING EXPENSE — ACCOUNT NO. 512

Date	Explanation	Post Ref.	Debit	Credit	Balance Debit	Balance Credit
			900 —		900 —	

TELEPHONE EXPENSE — ACCOUNT NO. 513

Date	Explanation	Post Ref.	Debit	Credit	Balance Debit	Balance Credit
	Paid Bill		210 —		210 —	

RENT EXPENSE — ACCOUNT NO. 514

Date	Explanation	Post Ref.	Debit	Credit	Balance Debit	Balance Credit
	Rent Expired (Used)		600 —		600 —	

SNOW SUPPLIES EXPENSE — ACCOUNT NO. 515

Date	Explanation	Post Ref.	Debit	Credit	Balance Debit	Balance Credit
			300 —		300 =	

PROBLEM 5A-3 OR PROBLEM 5B-3 (CONTINUED)

DEPRECIATION EXPENSE, OFFICE EQUIPMENT   ACCOUNT NO. 516

Date	Explanation	Post Ref.	Debit	Credit	Balance Debit	Balance Credit
			1 20		1 20 —	

DEPRECIATION EXPENSE, SNOW EQUIPMENT   ACCOUNT NO. 517

Date	Explanation	Post Ref.	Debit	Credit	Balance Debit	Balance Credit
			1 00		1 00	

PROBLEM 5A-3 OR PROBLEM 5B-3 (CONTINUED)

PETE'S PLOWING
INCOME STATEMENT
FOR MONTH ENDED JANUARY 31, 200X

Snow Plowing Fees Earned				20 0 0 0	—
Salaries Expense	1 9 9 0				
Advertising Expense	9 0 0	—			
Telephone Expense	2 1 0				
Rent Expense	6 0 0				
Snow Supplies Expense	3 0 0				
Depr. Expense, Office Equipment	1 2 0				
Depr. Expense, Snow Equipment	1 0 0				
	4 2 2 0		20 0 0 0	—
Net income	15 7 8 0			
	20 0 0 0		20 0 0 0	

PETE'S PLOWING
STATEMENT OF OWNER'S EQUITY
FOR MONTH ENDED JANUARY 31, 200X

PROBLEM 5A-3 OR PROBLEM 5B-3 (CONCLUDED)

PETE'S PLOWING
BALANCE SHEET
JANUARY 31, 200X

ASSETS

Cash	18000	
Acct Rec.	5000	
Prepaid Rent	1400	
Snow Supplies	400	
Office Equipment	7000	
Snow Equipment	6000	
		32600

LIABILITIES AND OWNER'S EQUITY

Liabilities		
Acct Payable	4500	
Salaries Payable	100	
Accm Depr. snow Equip	120	
Accm Depr. snow Supplies	100	
Liabilities		4910
Pete Mark Capital		14780
Net Income		15780

PROBLEM 5A-3 OR PROBLEM 5B-3 (CONCLUDED)

PETE'S PLOWING
POST-CLOSING TRIAL BALANCE
JANUARY 31, 200X

	Dr.	Cr.
Cash	12 6 9 0 —	
Acct. Rec.	5 0 0 0	
Prepaid Rent	1 4 0 0	
Snow Supplies	4 0 0	
Office Equipment	7 2 0 0	
Accm Snow Supplies Ex		1 0 0 —
Accm Office Equipment		1 2 0 —
Acct Payable		4 5 0 0 —
Salaries Payable		1 9 0 —
Pete Mack Capital		14 7 8 0 —
Snow Equipment	6 0 0 0	

CHAPTER 5
SUMMARY PRACTICE TEST:
THE ACCOUNTING CYCLE COMPLETED:
ADJUSTING, CLOSING, AND
THE POST-CLOSING TRIAL BALANCE

Part I Instructions

Fill in the blank(s) to complete the statement.

1. Income summary is _____ by the end of the period.
2. Revenue, Expenses, and Withdrawals are examples of _temporary accounts_.
3. _____ in temporary accounts will not be carried over to the next accounting period.
4. After closing entries are posted, owner's Capital in the ledger will contain the _____ _____.
5. Revenue is closed to Income Summary by a _____ to each revenue account and a _____ to Income Summary.
6. Expenses are closed to Income Summary by _____ the individual expenses and _____ Income Summary.
7. If the balance of Income Summary is a credit, it will be closed by _____ Income Summary and _____ owner's Capital.
8. The balance of Withdrawals is closed by a _____ and the amount transferred to owner's Capital by a _____.
9. At the end of the closing process, all temporary accounts in the ledger will have a _____ balance.
10. The _____ _____ _____ contains a list of permanent accounts after the adjusting and closing entries have been posted to the ledger from a journal.
11. Closing entries can be prepared from a _____.
12. After closing entries are posted, Income Summary will have a _____ balance.
13. Journalizing adjustments can be done from the _____.
14. Cash, Equipment, and Supplies are not part of the _____ process.
15. Income Summary is a _____ account.

Part II Instructions

The following is a chart of accounts for Jim's Fix-it Shop. From the chart, indicate in Column B (by account number) which accounts will be debited or credited as related to the transactions in Column A.

CHART OF ACCOUNTS

ASSETS	OWNER'S EQUITY
112 Cash	340 J. Fix, Capital
114 Accounts Receivable	341 J. Fix, Withdrawals
116 Prepaid Rent	342 Income Summary
118 Fix-It Supplies	
120 Truck	REVENUE
121 Accumulated Depreciation, Truck	450 Fix-It Fees Earned
LIABILITIES	EXPENSES
230 Accounts Payable	560 Salaries
232 Salaries Payable	562 Advertising
	564 Rent
	566 Fix-It Supplies
	568 Depreciation Expense, Truck

	COLUMN A	COLUMN B Debit(s)	Credit(s)
1.	Closed balance in revenue account to Income Summary.	_____	_____
2.	Closed balance in individual expenses to Income Summary	_____	_____
3.	Closed balance in Income Summary to owner's Capital. (Assume that it is a net income.)	_____	_____
4.	Closed Withdrawals to owner's Capital.	_____	_____
5.	Recorded Fix-It supplies used up.	_____	_____
6.	Recorded depreciation on truck.	_____	_____
7.	Brought Salaries Expense up to date (an adjustment).	_____	_____

Part III Instructions

Answer true or false to the following statements.

1. All companies journalize and post closing entries before the end of their calendar year.
2. Adjustments are journalized before preparing the worksheet.
3. Closing entries can only clear permanent accounts.
4. Income summary is a temporary account.
5. Interim statements can be prepared from worksheets.
6. To clear expenses in the closing process, a compound entry is appropriate.
7. Withdrawals is a permanent account.
8. Income Summary helps update withdrawals.

9. Accumulated Depreciation is a temporary account.

10. Cash, Rent Expense, and Accounts Receivable need to be closed at the end of the period.

11. Closing entries do not relate to the worksheet.

12. Revenue is closed by a credit.

13. Expenses are placed on the debit side of the Income Summary account.

14. A post-closing trial balance closely resembles the ending balance sheet.

15. Accumulated Depreciation never has to be adjusted.

16. Interim statements are always prepared monthly.

17. A post-closing trial balance is prepared before adjustments are journalized.

18. Income Summary is shown on the balance sheet.

19. The process of closing entries will help update owner's Capital.

20. An increase in Income Summary is a debit.

21. An increase in Income Summary is a credit.

22. The income statement is listed in terms of debits and credits.

23. Closing updates only permanent accounts.

24. The completion of financial statements means that the Capital account in the ledger has been updated.

25. Withdrawals is closed to Income Summary.

SOLUTIONS TO SUMMARY PRACTICE TEST

Part I

1.	closed	9.	zero
2.	temporary accounts	10.	post-closing trial balance
3.	balances	11.	worksheet
4.	ending figure (balance)	12.	zero
5.	debit, credit	13.	worksheet
6.	crediting, debiting	14.	closing
7.	debiting, crediting	15.	temporary
8.	credit, debit		

Part II

	Debit	Credit
1.	450	342
2.	342	560, 562, 564, 566, 568
3.	342	340
4.	340	341
5.	566	118
6.	568	121
7.	560	232

Part III

1. false	**7.** false	**13.** true	**19.** true	**25.** false
2. false	**8.** false	**14.** true	**20.** false	
3. false	**9.** false	**15.** false	**21.** false	
4. true	**10.** false	**16.** false	**22.** false	
5. true	**11.** false	**17.** false	**23.** false	
6. true	**12.** false	**18.** false	**24.** false	

CONTINUING PROBLEM FOR CHAPTER 5

SANCHEZ COMPUTER CENTER
GENERAL JOURNAL

PAGE 2

Date	Account Titles and Description	PR	Dr.	Cr.

CASH   ACCOUNT NO. 1000

Date		Explanation	Post Ref.	Debit	Credit	Balance	
						Debit	Credit
9/30	0X	Balance forward	✔			1 6 4 5 00	

ACCOUNTS RECEIVABLE   ACCOUNT NO. 1020

Date		Explanation	Post Ref.	Debit	Credit	Balance	
						Debit	Credit
9/30	0X	Balance forward	✔			2 6 0 0 00	

PREPAID RENT   ACCOUNT NO. 1025

Date		Explanation	Post Ref.	Debit	Credit	Balance	
						Debit	Credit
9/30	0X	Balance forward	✔			1 2 0 0 00	

SUPPLIES   ACCOUNT NO. 1030

Date		Explanation	Post Ref.	Debit	Credit	Balance	
						Debit	Credit
9/30	0X	Balance forward	✔			4 5 0 00	

Name _____ Class _____ Date _____

COMPUTER SHOP EQUIPMENT   ACCOUNT NO. <u>1080</u>

Date		Explanation	Post Ref.	Debit	Credit	Balance Debit	Balance Credit
9/30	0X	Balance forward	✔			2 4 0 0 00	

ACCUMULATED DEPRECIATION, COMPUTER SHOP EQUIPMENTACCOUNT NO. <u>1081</u>

Date	Explanation	Post Ref.	Debit	Credit	Balance Debit	Balance Credit

OFFICE EQUIPMENT   ACCOUNT NO. <u>1090</u>

Date		Explanation	Post Ref.	Debit	Credit	Balance Debit	Balance Credit
9/30	0X	Balance forward	✔			6 0 0 00	

ACCUMULATED DEPRECIATION, OFFICE EQUIPMENT   ACCOUNT NO. <u>1091</u>

Date	Explanation	Post Ref.	Debit	Credit	Balance Debit	Balance Credit

ACCOUNTS PAYABLE
ACCOUNT NO. 2000

Date		Explanation	Post Ref.	Debit	Credit	Balance	
						Debit	Credit
9/30	0X	Balance forward	✔				2 1 0 00

T. FREEDMAN, CAPITAL
ACCOUNT NO. 3000

Date		Explanation	Post Ref.	Debit	Credit	Balance	
						Debit	Credit
9/30	0X	Balance forward	✔				4 5 0 0 00

T. FREEDMAN, WITHDRAWALS
ACCOUNT NO. 3010

Date		Explanation	Post Ref.	Debit	Credit	Balance	
						Debit	Credit
9/30	0X	Balance forward	✔			1 0 0 00	

INCOME SUMMARY   ACCOUNT NO. 3020

Date		Explanation	Post Ref.	Debit	Credit	Balance	
						Debit	Credit

SERVICE REVENUE   ACCOUNT NO. 4000

Date		Explanation	Post Ref.	Debit	Credit	Balance	
						Debit	Credit
9/30	0X	Balance forward	✔				6 6 8 5 00

ADVERTISING EXPENSE   ACCOUNT NO. 5010

Date		Explanation	Post Ref.	Debit	Credit	Balance	
						Debit	Credit
9/30	0X	Balance forward	✔			1 4 0 0 00	

RENT EXPENSE   ACCOUNT NO. 5020

Date		Explanation	Post Ref.	Debit	Credit	Balance	
						Debit	Credit
9/30	0X	Balance forward	✔			4 0 0 00	

UTILITIES EXPENSE   ACCOUNT NO. 5030

Date		Explanation	Post Ref.	Debit	Credit	Balance	
						Debit	Credit
9/30	0X	Balance forward	✔			1 8 0 00	

PHONE EXPENSE   ACCOUNT NO. 5040

Date		Explanation	Post Ref.	Debit	Credit	Balance	
						Debit	Credit
9/30	0X	Balance forward	✔			2 2 0 00	

SUPPLIES EXPENSE   ACCOUNT NO. 5050

Date		Explanation	Post Ref.	Debit	Credit	Balance	
						Debit	Credit

INSURANCE EXPENSE   ACCOUNT NO. 5060

Date		Explanation	Post Ref.	Debit	Credit	Balance	
						Debit	Credit
9/30	0X	Balance forward	✔			1 5 0 00	

POSTAGE EXPENSE   **ACCOUNT NO. 5070**

Date		Explanation	Post Ref.	Debit	Credit	Balance	
						Debit	Credit
9/30	0X	Balance forward	✔			5 0 00	

DEPRECIATION EXPENSE C.S. EQUIPMENT   **ACCOUNT NO. 5080**

Date		Explanation	Post Ref.	Debit	Credit	Balance	
						Debit	Credit

DEPRECIATION EXPENSE OFFICE EQUIPMENT   **ACCOUNT NO. 5090**

Date		Explanation	Post Ref.	Debit	Credit	Balance	
						Debit	Credit

SANCHEZ COMPUTER CENTER
POST-CLOSING TRIAL BALANCE
SEPTEMBER 30, 200X

		Dr.			Cr.		

MINI PRACTICE SET
SULLIVAN REALTY

SULLIVAN REALTY
GENERAL JOURNAL

Date	Account Titles and Description	PR	Dr.	Cr.

MINI PRACTICE SET
SULLIVAN REALTY

SULLIVAN REALTY
GENERAL JOURNAL

PAGE 2

Date	Account Titles and Description	PR	Dr.	Cr.

MINI PRACTICE SET
SULLIVAN REALTY

SULLIVAN REALTY
GENERAL JOURNAL

PAGE 3

Date	Account Titles and Description	PR	Dr.	Cr.

MINI PRACTICE SET
SULLIVAN REALTY

SULLIVAN REALTY
GENERAL JOURNAL

Date	Account Titles and Description	PR	Dr.	Cr.

MINI PRACTICE SET
SULLIVAN REALTY

SULLIVAN REALTY
GENERAL JOURNAL

Date	Account Titles and Description	PR	Dr.	Cr.

MINI PRACTICE SET
SULLIVAN REALTY

SULLIVAN REALTY
GENERAL JOURNAL

PAGE 6

Date	Account Titles and Description	PR	Dr.	Cr.

MINI PRACTICE SET
SULLIVAN REALTY

CASH   **ACCOUNT NO. 111**

Date	Explanation	Post Ref.	Debit	Credit	Balance Debit	Balance Credit

MINI PRACTICE SET
SULLIVAN REALTY

ACCOUNTS RECEIVABLE　　　　ACCOUNT NO. 112

Date	Explanation	Post Ref.	Debit	Credit	Balance	
					Debit	Credit

PREPAID RENT　　　　ACCOUNT NO. 114

Date	Explanation	Post Ref.	Debit	Credit	Balance	
					Debit	Credit

OFFICE SUPPLIES　　　　ACCOUNT NO. 115

Date	Explanation	Post Ref.	Debit	Credit	Balance	
					Debit	Credit

OFFICE EQUIPMENT　　　　ACCOUNT NO. 121

Date	Explanation	Post Ref.	Debit	Credit	Balance	
					Debit	Credit

MINI PRACTICE SET: SULLIVAN REALTY

ACCUMULATED DEPRECIATION, OFFICE EQUIPMENT   ACCOUNT NO. 122

Date	Explanation	Post Ref.	Debit	Credit	Balance Debit	Balance Credit

AUTOMOBILE   ACCOUNT NO. 123

Date	Explanation	Post Ref.	Debit	Credit	Balance Debit	Balance Credit

ACCUMULATED DEPRECIATION, AUTOMOBILE   ACCOUNT NO. 124

Date	Explanation	Post Ref.	Debit	Credit	Balance Debit	Balance Credit

ACCOUNTS PAYABLE   ACCOUNT NO. 211

Date	Explanation	Post Ref.	Debit	Credit	Balance Debit	Balance Credit

SALARIES PAYABLE   ACCOUNT NO. 212

Date	Explanation	Post Ref.	Debit	Credit	Balance Debit	Balance Credit

MINI PRACTICE SET
SULLIVAN REALTY

JOHN SULLIVAN, CAPITAL   ACCOUNT NO. 311

Date	Explanation	Post Ref.	Debit	Credit	Balance Debit	Balance Credit

JOHN SULLIVAN, WITHDRAWALS   ACCOUNT NO. 312

Date	Explanation	Post Ref.	Debit	Credit	Balance Debit	Balance Credit

INCOME SUMMARY   ACCOUNT NO. 313

Date	Explanation	Post Ref.	Debit	Credit	Balance Debit	Balance Credit

MINI PRACTICE SET
SULLIVAN REALTY

COMMISSIONS EARNED   ACCOUNT NO. 411

Date		Explanation	Post Ref.	Debit	Credit	Balance	
						Debit	Credit

RENT EXPENSE   ACCOUNT NO. 511

Date		Explanation	Post Ref.	Debit	Credit	Balance	
						Debit	Credit

SALARIES EXPENSE   ACCOUNT NO. 512

Date		Explanation	Post Ref.	Debit	Credit	Balance	
						Debit	Credit

MINI PRACTICE SET
SULLIVAN REALTY

GAS EXPENSE ACCOUNT NO. 513

Date		Explanation	Post Ref.	Debit	Credit	Balance	
						Debit	Credit

REPAIRS EXPENSE ACCOUNT NO. 514

Date		Explanation	Post Ref.	Debit	Credit	Balance	
						Debit	Credit

TELEPHONE EXPENSE ACCOUNT NO. 515

Date		Explanation	Post Ref.	Debit	Credit	Balance	
						Debit	Credit

ADVERTISING EXPENSE ACCOUNT NO. 516

Date		Explanation	Post Ref.	Debit	Credit	Balance	
						Debit	Credit

MINI PRACTICE SET
SULLIVAN REALTY

OFFICE SUPPLIES EXPENSE ACCOUNT NO. 517

Date	Explanation	Post Ref.	Debit	Credit	Balance Debit	Balance Credit

DEPRECIATION EXPENSE, OFFICE EQUIPMENT ACCOUNT NO. 518

Date	Explanation	Post Ref.	Debit	Credit	Balance Debit	Balance Credit

DEPRECIATION EXPENSE, AUTOMOBILE ACCOUNT NO. 519

Date	Explanation	Post Ref.	Debit	Credit	Balance Debit	Balance Credit

MISCELLANEOUS EXPENSE ACCOUNT NO. 524

Date	Explanation	Post Ref.	Debit	Credit	Balance Debit	Balance Credit

MINI PRACTICE SET
SULLIVAN REALTY

SULLIVAN REALTY
INCOME STATEMENT
FOR MONTH ENDED JUNE 30, 200X

COMPREHENSIVE REVIEW PROBLEM:
SULLIVAN REALTY

Use blank fold-out worksheets located at the end of this text.

MINI PRACTICE SET
SULLIVAN REALTY

SULLIVAN REALTY
STATEMENT OF OWNER'S EQUITY
FOR MONTH ENDED JUNE 30, 200X

MINI PRACTICE SET
SULLIVAN REALTY

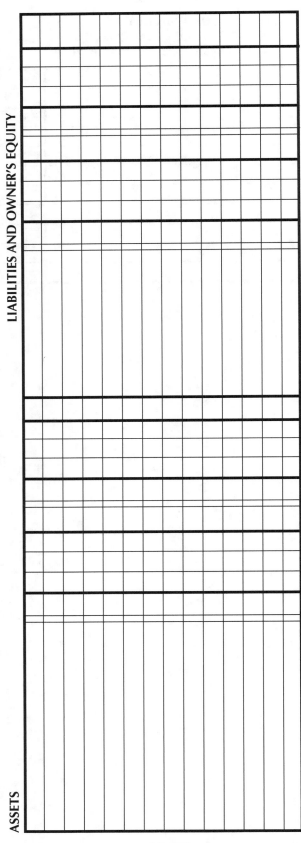

SULLIVAN REALTY
BALANCE SHEET
JUNE 30, 200X

ASSETS

LIABILITIES AND OWNER'S EQUITY

MINI PRACTICE SET
SULLIVAN REALTY

SULLIVAN REALTY
POST-CLOSING TRIAL BALANCE
JUNE 30, 200X

		Dr.		Cr.	

MINI PRACTICE SET
SULLIVAN REALTY

SULLIVAN REALTY
INCOME STATEMENT
FOR MONTH ENDED JULY 31, 200X

MINI PRACTICE SET
SULLIVAN REALTY

SULLIVAN REALTY
STATEMENT OF OWNER'S EQUITY
FOR MONTH ENDED JULY 31, 200X

**MINI PRACTICE SET
SULLIVAN REALTY**

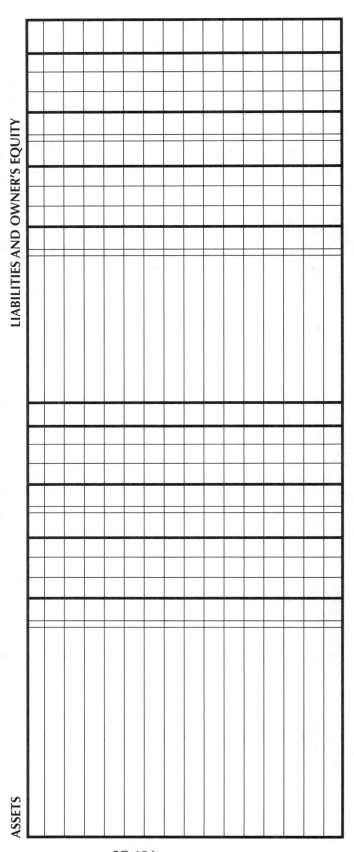

ASSETS

SULLIVAN REALTY
BALANCE SHEET
JULY 31, 200X

LIABILITIES AND OWNER'S EQUITY

MINI PRACTICE SET
SULLIVAN REALTY

SULLIVAN REALTY
POST-CLOSING TRIAL BALANCE
JULY 31, 200X

	Dr.	Cr.

BANKING PROCEDURES AND CONTROL OF CASH

6

SELF-REVIEW QUIZ 6-1

Situation	Add to Bank Balance	Deduct from Bank Balance	Add to Checkbook Balance	Deduct from Checkbook Balance
1				
2				
3				
4				
5				
6				
7				
8				

SELF-REVIEW QUIZ 6-2

PAGE 6

Date	Account Titles and Description	PR	Dr.	Cr.

AUXILIARY PETTY CASH RECORD

Date	Voucher No.	Description	Receipts	Payment	Category of Payment				
					Delivery Expense	General Expense	Sundry Account		Amount

CHAPTER 6
SET A   **CLASSROOM DEMONSTRATION EXERCISES**

1.

   A. _____   E. _____
   B. _____   F. _____
   C. _____
   D. _____

2.

3. _____   _____   _____   _____

JUNE CO.
BANK RECONCILIATION
MAY 31, 200X

Checkbook	Bank

4.

   A. _____ _____ _____   E. _____ _____ _____
   B. _____ _____ _____   F. _____ _____ _____
   C. _____ _____ _____
   D. _____ _____ _____

5.

6.

CHAPTER 6
SET B   **CLASSROOM DEMONSTRATION EXERCISES**

1.
   A. _____   E. _____
   B. _____   F. _____
   C. _____
   D. _____

2.

3.   _____   _____   _____   _____

JUNE CO.
BANK RECONCILIATION
MAY 31, 200X

<u>Checkbook</u>	<u>Bank</u>

4.
   A. _____ _____ _____   E. _____ _____ _____
   B. _____ _____ _____   F. _____ _____ _____
   C. _____ _____ _____
   D. _____ _____ _____

5.

6.

FORMS FOR EXERCISES

6-1.

LANG CO.
BANK RECONCILIATION AS OF JULY 31, 200X

CHECKBOOK BALANCE		BALANCE PER BANK	
Ending Checkbook Balance	_____	Ending Bank Statement Balance	_____
Deduct:	_____	Add:	_____
Bank Service Charge	_____	Deposit in Transit	_____
	_____		_____
	_____	Deduct:	_____
	_____	Outstanding Checks	_____
	_____		_____
Reconciled Balance	_____	Reconciled Balance	_____

6-2.

6-3.

EXERCISES (CONTINUED)

6-4.

6-5.

      Beg. Change Fund
+Cash Register Total
=Cash should have on hand
−Counted Cash
= Cash Shortage

END OF CHAPTER PROBLEMS

PROBLEM 6A-1 OR PROBLEM 6B-1

ABLE.COM
BANK RECONCILIATION AS OF JULY 31, 200X

BALANCE PER BANK

Bank Statement Balance

Add: _____

Deduct: _____

_____

Reconciled Balance   _____

CHECKBOOK BALANCE

Checkbook Balance

Add:

_____

Deduct:

_____

Reconciled Balance   _____

PROBLEM 6A-1 OR PROBLEM 6B-1 (CONCLUDED)

Date	Account Titles and Description	PR	Dr.	Cr.
	Bank Balance			6 6 0 0
112	Check outstanding		1 0 0 0	
130	check outstanding			
	Deposit in transit			1 1 0 0
	ATM gas purchase		2 3	
			3 5	
	Collection note			9 1 0
			0	
	Balance			

PROBLEM 6A-2 OR PROBLEM 6B-2

LOWELL NATIONAL BANK
RIO MEAN BRAND
BUGNA, TEXAS   TELEPHONE 555-8311

This form is provided to help you balance your bank statement. If no errors are reported to auditors in ten days, the account will be considered correct.

Please notify us of any change in address.

Checks outstanding
(not charged to account)

Check No.	Amount
Total	

Sort the checks numerically or by date issued.
Check off on the stubs of your checkbook each check paid by bank.
List the numbers and amounts of checks still outstanding in the space provided at the left.
Verify the deposits in your checkbook with deposits credited on this statement. Bank balance show on this statement $_____
Plus: Deposits not
   credited on this statement $_____
     Subtotal $_____
Less: Checks outstanding $_____
Balance $_____

If your checkbook does not agree, enter any necessary adjustments:
_____
_____
_____
Correct checkbook balance $_____

PROBLEM 6A-2 OR PROBLEM 6B-2 (CONCLUDED)

GENERAL JOURNAL

Date	Account Titles and Description	PR	Dr.	Cr.

Name _____ Class _____ Date _____

PROBLEM 6A-3 OR PROBLEM 6B-3

MERRY CO.
GENERAL JOURNAL

Date	Account Titles and Description	PR	Dr.		Cr.	
	Petty Cash		1 0 0 —			
	Cash check #				1 0 0 —	
	Postage Expense		1 5			
	Supplies Expense		2 0			
	Supplies Expense		1 8			
	Postage Expense		1 4			
	donation Expense		9			
	Cash				7 6 —	
	Replenishment					
	Petty Cash		2 4			

PROBLEM 6A-3 OR PROBLEM 6B-3 (CONCLUDED)

MERRY CO.
AUXILIARY PETTY CASH RECORD

Date	Voucher No.	Description	Receipts	Payment	Postage Expense	Office Supplies Expense	Account (Sundry)	Amount (Sundry)
4/1		Establishment	100					
4/5	1	Postage		15	15			
8	2	Supplies		26		26		
17	3	Supplies		18		18		
24	4	Postal		14	14			
26	5	donation		9			MIS	9
		Total	100	76	29	38		9
		End balance		24				
			100	100				
		Ending bal	24					
		Replenishment	76					
		New Bal	100					

PROBLEM 6A-4 OR PROBLEM 6B-4

LOGAN CO.
GENERAL JOURNAL

Date	Account Titles and Description	PR	Dr.	Cr.

PROBLEM 6A-4 OR PROBLEM 6B-4

LOGAN CO.
AUXILIARY PETTY CASH RECORD

Date	Voucher No.	Description	Receipts	Payment	Postage Expense	Delivery Expense	Category of Payment — Account	Sundry Amount
Oct. 5	1	Establishment	150					
5	2	Postage		24	24			
18	3	Delivery		12		12		
18	4	Donation		8			Church	8
17	5	Postage Delivery		18	9	18		
27	6	Supplies		18			Supplies	18
28	7	Postage		14	14			
		Total		103	47	30	over & shortage	3
				47				29
		End Bal.	47	150				
		Replenishment	63					
		New bal.	150					

CHAPTER 6
SUMMARY PRACTICE TEST
BANKING PROCEDURES AND CONTROL OF CASH

Part I Instructions

Fill in the blank(s) to complete the statement.

1. _____ _____ limit any further negotiations of a check.
2. Deposits in transit are _____ to the bank balance.
3. All adjustments to the checkbook balance in the reconciliation process will require _____ _____.
4. Petty cash is an _____ found on the balance sheet.
5. The auxiliary petty cash record is not a _____.
6. A _____ _____ is an asset used to make change for customer.
7. A cash overage will be _____ _____ on the income statement.
8. _____ _____ represents checks not processed by the bank at the time the bank statement was prepared.
9. When a bank debits your account, your balance will _____.
10. _____ is a procedure whereby the bank does not return the processed checks.

Part II Instructions

Indicate which of the following procedures are involved in each of the transactions below

a. Recorded in General Journal
b. Recorded in both general journal and auxiliary petty cash record
c. Recorded only in auxiliary petty cash record
d. New check is written
e. Account petty cash is increased

1. EXAMPLE: Check issued to establish petty cash   <u>b,d,e</u>
2. Paid donation from petty cash   _____
3. Paid postage from petty cash   _____
4. Paid past purchases previously charged   _____
5. Paid for business luncheon with petty cash   _____
6. Issued check to pay for office supplies   _____
7. Replenished petty cash   _____
8. Paid local donation from petty cash   _____
9. Paid for past purchases bought on account   _____
10. Replenished petty cash   _____

Part III Instructions

Answer true or false to the following statements.

1. Checks outstanding have reached the bank but have not been recorded in the checkbook.
2. Petty cash is a liability found on the balance sheet.
3. Checks returned from the bank are placed in alphabetical order.
4. The General Journal has a record of all checks written.
5. Bank service charges represent an expense to the business.
6. The bank statement is the same as the bank reconciliation.
7. The balance in the company cash account will always equal the bank balance before the bank statement is received.
8. Deposit slips are needed in writing checks.
9. The signature must be presented when cashing a check.
10. The auxiliary petty cash record is posted monthly.
11. The petty cash account has a debit balance.
12. Replenishment of petty cash requires a new check.
13. The expenses paid from petty cash are journalized at time of replenishment.
14. Internal control only affects large companies.
15. A petty cash voucher records the expense into the ledger.
16. The petty cash fund must be replenished monthly.
17. The petty cash voucher identifies the account that will be charged.
18. The establishment of petty cash may require some judgment as to the amount of petty cash needed.
19. EFT is the same as safekeeping.
20. The drawer is the person who receives the check.
21. A debit memo will increase the depositor's balance.
22. A change fund uses only one denomination.
23. The payer is the person or company the check is payable to.

Part IV Instructions

Based on the following situation, prepare a bank reconciliation.
The checkbook balance of Moore Company is $3,763.08. The bank statement shows a bank balance of $6,480. The bank statement shows interest earned of $42 and a service charge of $29.76. There is a deposit in transit of $2,558.22. Outstanding checks total $3,762.90. The bank collected a note for Moore for $4,200. Moore Company forgot to deduct a check for $2,700 during the month.

SOLUTIONS TO SUMMARY PRACTICE TEST

PART I

1. restrictive endorsements
2. added
3. journal entries
4. asset
5. journal
6. change fund
7. miscellaneous income
8. checks outstanding
9. decrease
10. safekeeping

Part II

1. b, d, e
2. c
3. c
4. a, d
5. c
6. a, d
7. b, d
8. c
9. a, d
10. b, d

Part III

1. false
2. false
3. false
4. false
5. true
6. false
7. false
8. false
9. true
10. false
11. true
12. true
13. true
14. false
15. false
16. false
17. true
18. true
19. false
20. false
21. false
22. false
23. false

Part IV

MOORE CO.			BANK BALANCE	
Checkbook Balance		$3,763.08	Bank Balance	$6,480.00
ADD:			ADD:	
			Deposit	
Interest	$ 42		in Transit	2,558.22
Collection of note	4,200	4,242.00		$9,038.22
		8,005.08		
DEDUCT:			DEDUCT:	
Service Chg.	$ 29.76		Check outstanding	$3,762.90
Error	2,700.00	2,729.76		
Reconciled Balance		$5,275.32	Reconciled Balance	$5,275.32

CONTINUING PROBLEM FOR CHAPTER 6

SANCHEZ COMPUTER CENTER
GENERAL JOURNAL

PAGE 3

Date	Account Titles and Description	PR	Dr.	Cr.

CASH   **ACCOUNT NO. 1000**

Date		Explanation	Post Ref.	Debit	Credit	Balance Debit	Balance Credit
9/30	0X	Balance forward	✔			1 6 4 5 00	

PETTY CASH   **ACCOUNT NO. 1010**

Date		Explanation	Post Ref.	Debit	Credit	Balance Debit	Balance Credit

ACCOUNTS RECEIVABLE   ACCOUNT NO. 1020

Date		Explanation	Post Ref.	Debit	Credit	Balance Debit	Balance Credit
9/30	0X	Balance forward	✔			2 6 0 0 00	

PREPAID RENT   ACCOUNT NO. 1025

Date		Explanation	Post Ref.	Debit	Credit	Balance Debit	Balance Credit
9/30	0X	Balance forward	✔			4 0 0 00	

SUPPLIES   ACCOUNT NO. 1030

Date		Explanation	Post Ref.	Debit	Credit	Balance Debit	Balance Credit
9/30	0X	Balance forward	✔			9 0 00	

COMPUTER SHOP EQUIPMENT   ACCOUNT NO. 1080

Date		Explanation	Post Ref.	Debit	Credit	Balance Debit	Balance Credit
9/30	0X	Balance forward	✔			2 4 0 0 00	

ACCUMULATED DEPRECIATION, COMPUTER SHOP EQUIPMENT   ACCOUNT NO. 1081

Date		Explanation	Post Ref.	Debit	Credit	Balance	
						Debit	Credit
9/30	0X	Balance forward	✔				9 9

OFFICE EQUIPMENT   ACCOUNT NO. 1090

Date		Explanation	Post Ref.	Debit	Credit	Balance	
						Debit	Credit
9/30	0X	Balance forward	✔			6 0 0 00	

ACCUMULATED DEPRECIATION, OFFICE EQUIPMENT   ACCOUNT NO. 1091

Date		Explanation	Post Ref.	Debit	Credit	Balance	
						Debit	Credit
9/30	0X	Balance forward	✔				2 0 00

ACCOUNTS PAYABLE   ACCOUNT NO. 2000

Date		Explanation	Post Ref.	Debit	Credit	Balance	
						Debit	Credit
9/30	0X	Balance forward	✔				2 1 0 00

T. FREEDMAN, CAPITAL   **ACCOUNT NO. 3000**

Date		Explanation	Post Ref.	Debit	Credit	Balance		
							Debit	Credit
9/30	0X	Balance forward	✔					7 4 0 6 00

T. FREEDMAN, WITHDRAWALS   **ACCOUNT NO. 3010**

Date		Explanation	Post Ref.	Debit	Credit	Balance		
							Debit	Credit

INCOME SUMMARY   **ACCOUNT NO. 3020**

Date		Explanation	Post Ref.	Debit	Credit	Balance		
							Debit	Credit

SERVICE REVENUE   ACCOUNT NO. 4000

Date	Explanation	Post Ref.	Debit	Credit	Balance	
					Debit	Credit

ADVERTISING EXPENSE   ACCOUNT NO. 5010

Date	Explanation	Post Ref.	Debit	Credit	Balance	
					Debit	Credit

RENT EXPENSE   ACCOUNT NO. 5020

Date	Explanation	Post Ref.	Debit	Credit	Balance	
					Debit	Credit

UTILITIES EXPENSE   ACCOUNT NO. 5030

Date		Explanation	Post Ref.	Debit	Credit	Balance	
						Debit	Credit

PHONE EXPENSE   ACCOUNT NO. 5040

Date		Explanation	Post Ref.	Debit	Credit	Balance	
						Debit	Credit

SUPPLIES EXPENSE   ACCOUNT NO. 5050

Date		Explanation	Post Ref.	Debit	Credit	Balance	
						Debit	Credit

INSURANCE EXPENSE   ACCOUNT NO. 5060

Date		Explanation	Post Ref.	Debit	Credit	Balance	
						Debit	Credit

POSTAGE EXPENSE ACCOUNT NO. <u>5070</u>

Date		Explanation	Post Ref.	Debit	Credit	Balance	
						Debit	Credit

DEPRECIATION EXPENSE, COMPUTER SHOP EQUIPMENT ACCOUNT NO. <u>5080</u>

Date		Explanation	Post Ref.	Debit	Credit	Balance	
						Debit	Credit

DEPRECIATION EXPENSE, OFFICE EQUIPMENT ACCOUNT NO. <u>5090</u>

Date		Explanation	Post Ref.	Debit	Credit	Balance	
						Debit	Credit

MISCELLANEOUS EXPENSE ACCOUNT NO. <u>5100</u>

Date		Explanation	Post Ref.	Debit	Credit	Balance	
						Debit	Credit

SANCHEZ COMPUTER CENTER
TRIAL BALANCE
OCTOBER 31, 200X

AUXILIARY PETTY CASH RECORD

Date	Voucher No.	Description	Receipts	Payment	Category of Payment				
					Postage Expense	Supplies Expense	Account	Sundry Amount	

SANCHEZ COMPUTER CENTER
BANK RECONCILIATION AS OF SEPTEMBER 30, 200X

BALANCE PER BANK

Bank Statement Balance

  Add: _____

  Deduct: _____

  _____

Reconciled Balance _____

CHECKBOOK BALANCE

Checkbook Balance

  Add:

  _____

  Deduct:

  _____

Reconciled Balance _____

PAYROLL CONCEPTS AND PROCEDURE— EMPLOYEE TAXES

SELF-REVIEW QUIZ 7-1

REGULAR EARNINGS

OVERTIME

GROSS EARNINGS

SELF-REVIEW QUIZ 7-2

FIT

SIT

FICA - OASDI

FICA - MEDICARE

NET PAY

SELF-REVIEW QUIZ 7-3

FICA - OASD1_____

FICA - Medicare_____

FUTA_____

SUTA_____

Name _____ Class _____ Date _____

FORMS FOR CHAPTER 7
SET A   **CLASSROOM DEMONSTRATION EXERCISES**

1. A. _____
    _____
    _____

    B. _____
    _____
    _____

2. _____
   _____
   _____
   _____
   _____

3. _____
   _____
   _____
   _____

4. A. _____ D. _____
    B. _____ E. _____
    C. _____ F. _____

5.
    A. _____
    B. _____
    C. _____
    D. _____

FORMS FOR CHAPTER 7
CLASSROOM DEMONSTRATION EXERCISES

SET B

1. A. _____
    _____
    _____

    B. _____
    _____
    _____

2. _____
    _____
    _____
    _____
    _____

3. _____
    _____
    _____
    _____

4. A. _____ D. _____
    B. _____ E. _____
    C. _____ F. _____

5.
    A. _____
    B. _____
    C. _____
    D. _____

Name _____ Class _____ Date _____

FORMS FOR EXERCISES

7-1.

Carmen _____

Jill _____
_____

Fred _____
_____

7-2.

Alvin   Angeline

_____   _____
_____   _____
_____   _____
_____   _____
_____   _____
_____   _____
_____   _____
_____   _____

7-3 _____
_____
_____
_____
_____

7-4. _____
_____
_____
_____
_____
_____

EXERCISES (CONTINUED)

7-5. _____
_____
_____
_____
_____

7-6. _____
_____
_____
_____
_____

7-7.

Employee	Weekly Pay	Weeks	Total	Taxable	Tax Rate	Tax

7-8. _____
_____
_____

END OF CHAPTER PROBLEMS

PROBLEM 7A-1 OR PROBLEM 7B-1

Employee	Hourly Rate	# of Hours Worked	Gross Earnings
A.			
B.			
C.			
D.			

A.   B.

C.   D.

PROBLEM 7A-2 OR PROBLEM 7B-2

Use the fold-out payroll register located at the end of this text.

PROBLEM 7A-3 OR PROBLEM 7B-3

Use the fold-out payroll register located at the end of this text.

PROBLEM 7A-4 OR PROBLEM 7B-4

Use the fold-out payroll register located at the end of this text.

CHAPTER 7
SUMMARY PRACTICE TEST:
PAYROLL CONCEPTS AND PROCEDURES—EMPLOYEE TAXES

PART I INSTRUCTIONS

Fill in the blank (s) to complete the statement.

1. The _____ _____ _____
   _____ states the maximum hours a worker will work at regular rate of pay.
2. Form _____ aids the employer in knowing how much to deduct for federal
   income tax.
3. The base for FICA-Medicare will _____ _____ from
   year to year.
4. _____ _____ of the employer's tax guide has
   tables available for deductions for FIT and FICA (OASDI and Medicare).
5. _____ _____ _____
   protects employees against losses due to injury or death incurred while on the job.
6. The two primary records used to keep track of payroll information are the _____ and _____.
7. The employer is responsible for paying for_____.
8. _____ is paid every two weeks.
9. A(n) _____ employee will only be paid for the hours actually worked.
10. An employer must pay FUTA on wages earned by each employee up to a maximum of $_____.

Part II Instructions

Answer true or false to the following.

1. The individual earnings record is updated from the general journal.
2. Employers only pay FUTA and SUTA.
3. Employers pay a higher FICA-OASDI tax rate than employees do.
4. Gross pay plus deductions equals net pay.
5. Form W-4 aids in calculating FICA-OASDI.
6. The employer will match the employee's contribution for FICA (OASDI and Medicare).
7. The maximum tax credit for state unemployment tax is .8%.
8. A company may have different types of employees.

9. The Wage-Bracket Table makes it more difficult to calculate the amount of deductions for FIT.

10. A calendar year has no effect on taxes for FICA-Social Security.

Part III Instructions

Complete the chart below (use table in text as needed). Use the following information: Before this payroll John Roll had earned $94,100. This week John earned $900 for the past two weeks. Assume a FICA rate of Social Security of 6.2% up to $94,200. Medicare, 1.45%. John is single, claiming one deduction. The state income tax is 7 percent.

| GROSS PAY | TAXABLE FICA | DEDUCTIONS | | FIT | SIT | NET PAY |
| | | FICA | | | | |
		Soc. Sec.	Med.			

CHAPTER 7
SOLUTIONS TO SUMMARY PRACTICE TEST

Part I

1. Fair Labors Standards Act
2. W-4
3. Not change
4. Circular E
5. Workers' Compensation Insurance
6. Payroll register and employee earnings record
7. FUTA (SUTA)
8. Biweekly payroll
9. Hourly
10. $7,000

Part II

1. false
2. true
3. false
4. false
5. false
6. true
7. false
8. true
9. false
10. false

Part III

FICA			
Social Security	$100 x .062 =	$ 6.20	
Medicare	900 x .0145 =	13.05	
FIT	by table	88.00	$900.00
SIT	900 x .07	63.00	− 170.25
Total deductions		$170.25	$729.75

CONTINUING PROBLEM FOR CHAPTER 7

SANCHEZ COMPUTER CENTER
GENERAL JOURNAL

Date	Account Titles and Description	PR	Dr.	Cr.

SANCHEZ COMPUTER CENTER
GENERAL JOURNAL

Date	Account Titles and Description	PR	Dr.	Cr.

CASH

ACCOUNT NO. 1000

Date		Explanation	Post Ref.	Debit	Credit	Balance				
						Debit			Credit	
10/31	0X	Balance forward	✔			4	2 9 3	00		

PETTY CASH

ACCOUNT NO. 1010

Date		Explanation	Post Ref.	Debit	Credit	Balance				
						Debit			Credit	
10/31	0X	Balance forward	✔			1	0 0	00		

ACCOUNTS RECEIVABLE

ACCOUNT NO. 1020

Date		Explanation	Post Ref.	Debit	Credit	Balance				
						Debit			Credit	
10/31	0X	Balance forward	✔			4	2 0 0	00		

PREPAID RENT   ACCOUNT NO. 1025

Date		Explanation	Post Ref.	Debit	Credit	Balance	
						Debit	Credit
10/31	0X	Balance forward	✔			1 6 0 0 00	

SUPPLIES   ACCOUNT NO. 1030

Date		Explanation	Post Ref.	Debit	Credit	Balance	
						Debit	Credit
10/31	0X	Balance forward	✔			9 0 00	

COMPUTER SHOP EQUIPMENT   ACCOUNT NO. 1080

Date		Explanation	Post Ref.	Debit	Credit	Balance	
						Debit	Credit
10/31	0X	Balance forward	✔			2 4 0 0 00	

ACCUMULATED DEPRECIATION, COMPUTER SHOP EQUIPMENT   ACCOUNT NO. 1081

Date		Explanation	Post Ref.	Debit	Credit	Balance	
						Debit	Credit
10/31	0X	Balance forward	✔				9 9 00

OFFICE EQUIPMENT

ACCOUNT NO. 1090

Date		Explanation	Post Ref.	Debit	Credit	Balance	
						Debit	Credit
10/31	0X	Balance forward	✔			6 0 0 00	

ACCUMULATED DEPRECIATION, OFFICE EQUIPMENT

ACCOUNT NO. 1091

Date		Explanation	Post Ref.	Debit	Credit	Balance	
						Debit	Credit
10/31	0X	Balance forward	✔				2 0 00

ACCOUNTS PAYABLE

ACCOUNT NO. 2000

Date		Explanation	Post Ref.	Debit	Credit	Balance	
						Debit	Credit
10/31	0X	Balance forward	✔				5 0 00

WAGES PAYABLE

ACCOUNT NO. 2010

Date		Explanation	Post Ref.	Debit	Credit	Balance	
						Debit	Credit

PARTIAL GENERAL LEDGER

FICA—OASDI PAYABLE   ACCOUNT NO. 2020

Date		Explanation	Post Ref.	Debit	Credit	Balance	
						Debit	Credit

FICA—MEDICARE PAYABLE   ACCOUNT NO. 2030

Date		Explanation	Post Ref.	Debit	Credit	Balance	
						Debit	Credit

FIT PAYABLE   ACCOUNT NO. 2040

Date		Explanation	Post Ref.	Debit	Credit	Balance	
						Debit	Credit

SIT PAYABLE   ACCOUNT NO. 2050

Date		Explanation	Post Ref.	Debit	Credit	Balance	
						Debit	Credit

T. FREEDMAN CAPITAL

ACCOUNT NO. **3000**

Date		Explanation	Post Ref.	Debit	Credit	Balance	
						Debit	Credit
10/31	0X	Balance forward	✔				7 4 0 6 00

T. FREEDMAN WITHDRAWALS

ACCOUNT NO.

Date		Explanation	Post Ref.	Debit	Credit	Balance	
						Debit	Credit
10/31	0X	Balance forward	✔			2 0 1 5 00	

SERVICE REVENUE

ACCOUNT NO. **4000**

Date		Explanation	Post Ref.	Debit	Credit	Balance	
						Debit	Credit
10/31	0X	Balance forward	✔				7 8 0 0 00

ADVERTISING EXPENSE

ACCOUNT NO. **5010**

Date		Explanation	Post Ref.	Debit	Credit	Balance	
						Debit	Credit

RENT EXPENSE

ACCOUNT NO. **5020**

Date		Explanation	Post Ref.	Debit	Credit	Balance	
						Debit	Credit

UTILITIES EXPENSE   ACCOUNT NO. <u>5030</u>

Date		Explanation	Post Ref.	Debit	Credit	Balance	
						Debit	Credit

PHONE EXPENSE   ACCOUNT NO. <u>5040</u>

Date		Explanation	Post Ref.	Debit	Credit	Balance	
						Debit	Credit

SUPPLIES EXPENSE   ACCOUNT NO. <u>5050</u>

Date		Explanation	Post Ref.	Debit	Credit	Balance	
						Debit	Credit
10/31	0X		✔			4 2 00	

INSURANCE EXPENSE   ACCOUNT NO. <u>5060</u>

Date		Explanation	Post Ref.	Debit	Credit	Balance	
						Debit	Credit

POSTAGE EXPENSE   ACCOUNT NO. <u>5070</u>

Date		Explanation	Post Ref.	Debit	Credit	Balance	
						Debit	Credit
10/31	0X	Balance forward	✔			2 5 00	

DEPRECIATION EXPENSE C. S. EQUIPMENT   ACCOUNT NO. 5080

Date		Explanation	Post Ref.	Debit	Credit	Balance	
						Debit	Credit

DEPRECIATION EXPENSE OFFICE EQUIPMENT   ACCOUNT NO. 5090

Date		Explanation	Post Ref.	Debit	Credit	Balance	
						Debit	Credit

MISCELLANEOUS EXPENSE   ACCOUNT NO. 5100

Date		Explanation	Post Ref.	Debit	Credit	Balance	
						Debit	Credit
10/31	0X	Balance forward	✔			1 0 00	

WAGES EXPENSE   ACCOUNT NO. 5110

Date		Explanation	Post Ref.	Debit	Credit	Balance	
						Debit	Credit

SANCHEZ COMPUTER CENTER
TRIAL BALANCE
NOVEMBER 30, 200X

		Dr.		Cr.	

THE EMPLOYER'S TAX RESPONSIBILITIES: PRINCIPLES AND PROCEDURES

SELF-REVIEW QUIZ 8-1

GENERAL JOURNAL

PAGE 1

Date	Account Titles and Description	PR	Dr.	Cr.

SELF-REVIEW QUIZ 8-2

1.

2.

SELF-REVIEW QUIZ 8-3

1. _____ 2. _____ 3. _____ 4. _____ 5. _____ 6. _____

SET A   **FORMS FOR CLASSROOM DEMONSTRATION EXERCISES**

1.

A.			
B.			
C.			
D.			
E.			

2.

A. _____

B. _____

C. _____

D. _____

3.

_____

_____

_____

_____

4.

A. _____

B. _____

C. _____

D. _____

E. _____

F. _____

G. _____

5.

A. _____

B. _____

C. _____

D. _____

E. _____

Name _____ Class _____ Date _____

SET B   **FORMS FOR CLASSROOM DEMONSTRATION EXERCISES**

1.

A.			
B.			
C.			
D.			
E.			

2.

A. _____

B. _____

C. _____

D. _____

3.

_____

_____

_____

_____

4.

A. _____

B. _____

C. _____

D. _____

E. _____

F. _____

G. _____

5.

A. _____

B. _____

C. _____

D. _____

E. _____

Name _____ Class _____ Date _____

FORMS FOR EXERCISES

8-1. See Chapter 7, 7-3 _____

_____

_____

_____

_____

_____

_____

_____

_____

_____

_____

8-2. See Chapter 7, 7-5 _____

_____

_____

_____

_____

_____

_____

_____

_____

_____

_____

8-3.

EXERCISES (CONTINUED)

8-4.

	1.0% SUTA	08% FUTA	
A	63.55	8.40	1050
B	45.90	7.20	900
C	51.00	8.00	1000
D	64.26	10.08	1260
E	80.58	12.64	1580
	214.71	33.68	

8-5.

8-6.

8-7.

8-8.

Name _____ Class _____ Date _____

END OF CHAPTER PROBLEMS

PROBLEM 8A-1 OR PROBLEM 8B-1

69.33

Employee	Allowance & Marital Status	Gross	FICA OASDI (6.2%)	FICA Medicare (1.45)	Federal Income Tax (pg 253)
A Eddie Janway	S 1	1,050	65.10	15.23	109
B Jan Kunz	S-0	900	55.80	13.05	107
C Julia Long	S-2	1000	62.00	14.50	84
D Mike Roald	S-0	1260	78.12	18.87	159
E Tom Valens	S-2	1580	97.96	22.91	176
			358.98	83.96	635

(2) SUTA—5.1% FUTA .8%

		Payroll Tax Expense				6	9	1	33		
		FICA OASDI Payable								3 5 8 98
		FICA Medicare Payable								8 3 96
		FUTA Payable								3 3 68
		SUTA Payable								2 1 4 71

SG-239

Name _SUTA · 1,148.55_   Class _____   Date _____

PROBLEM 8A-2 OR PROBLEM 8B-2

Date	Account Titles and Description	PR	Dr.	Cr.
Jan	Payroll Expense		6 7 9 23	
	FICA OASDI Payable			5 4 4 80
	FICA Medicare Payable			1 2 8 23
	FUTA Payable			1 1 60
	SUTA Payable			9 5 6 40
Feb	Payroll Expense			
	FICA OASDI Payable			
	FICA Medicare Payable			
	FUTA Payable			
	SUTA Payable			
Mar	Payroll Expense			
	FICA OASDI Payable			
	FICA Medicare Payable			
	FUTA Payable			
	SUTA Payable			

PROBLEM 8A-2 OR PROBLEM 8B-2 (CONCLUDED)   Tax liabilities

Date		Account Titles and Description	PR		Dr.				Cr.		

PROBLEM 8A-3 OR PROBLEM 8B-3

7972.90

Form **941 for 200X:** **Employer's QUARTERLY Federal Tax Return**
(Rev. January 2006)   Department of the Treasury — Internal Revenue Service

990106

OMB No. 1545-0029

(EIN)
Employer identification number `2 9 - 3 4 5 8 8 2 2`

Name *(not your trade name)* White Company

Trade name *(if any)*

Address 1 Square Street
Number / Street / Suite or room number
Marblehead   MA   01945
City   State ZIP code

Report for this Quarter ...
(Check one.)

- [✓] **1:** January, February, March
- [ ] **2:** April, May, June
- [ ] **3:** July, August, September
- [ ] **4:** October, November, December

Read the separate instructions before you fill out this form. Please type or print within the boxes.

Part 1: Answer these questions for this quarter.

1 Number of employees who received wages, tips, or other compensation for the pay period including: *Mar. 12* (Quarter 1), *June 12* (Quarter 2), *Sept. 12* (Quarter 3), *Dec. 12* (Quarter 4) **1** `3`

2 Wages, tips, and other compensation **2** `26,875.`

3 Total income tax withheld from wages, tips, and other compensation **3** `383861.00`

4 If no wages, tips, and other compensation are subject to social security or Medicare tax [ ] Check and go to line 6.

5 Taxable social security and Medicare wages and tips:

		Column 1		Column 2
5a Taxable social security wages		`26875.`	× .124 =	`3332.50`
5b Taxable social security tips		`.`	× .124 =	`.`
5c Taxable Medicare wages & tips		`26875.`	× .029 =	`779.40`

5d Total social security and Medicare taxes (*Column 2,* lines 5a + 5b + 5c = line 5d) **5d** `4111.90`

6 Total taxes before adjustments (lines 3 + 5d = line 6) **6** `7972.90`

7 **TAX ADJUSTMENTS** (Read the instructions for line 7 before completing lines 7a through 7h.):

7a Current quarter's fractions of cents `.`

7b Current quarter's sick pay `.`

7c Current quarter's adjustments for tips and group-term life insurance `.`

7d Current year's income tax withholding (attach Form 941c) `.`

7e Prior quarters' social security and Medicare taxes (attach Form 941c) `.`

7f Special additions to federal income tax (attach Form 941c) `.`

7g Special additions to social security and Medicare (attach Form 941c) `.`

7h **TOTAL ADJUSTMENTS** (Combine all amounts: lines 7a through 7g.) **7h** `.`

8 Total taxes after adjustments (Combine lines 6 and 7h.) **8** `.`

9 Advance earned income credit (EIC) payments made to employees **9** `.`

10 Total taxes after adjustment for advance EIC (line 8 – line 9 = line 10) **10** `.`

11 Total deposits for this quarter, including overpayment applied from a prior quarter **11** `.`

12 **Balance due** (If line 10 is more than line 11, write the difference here.) **12** `.`
Make checks payable to *United States Treasury.*

13 **Overpayment** (If line 11 is more than line 10, write the difference here.) `.` Check one [ ] Apply to next return. [ ] Send a refund.

► You **MUST** fill out both pages of this form and **SIGN** it.

Next ➡

For Privacy Act and Paperwork Reduction Act Notice, see the back of the Payment Voucher.   Cat. No. 17001Z   Form **941** (Rev. 1-2006)

PROBLEM 8A-3 OR PROBLEM 8B-3

990206

Name (not your trade name)	Employer identification number (EIN)

Part 2: Tell us about your deposit schedule and tax liability for this quarter.

If you are unsure about whether you are a monthly schedule depositor or a semiweekly schedule depositor, see *Pub. 15 (Circular E)*, section 11.

14 ☐ ☐ Write the state abbreviation for the state where you made your deposits OR write "MU" if you made your deposits in *multiple* states.

15 Check one: ☐ Line 10 is less than $2,500. Go to Part 3.

☐ You were a monthly schedule depositor for the entire quarter. Fill out your tax liability for each month. Then go to Part 3.

Tax liability: Month 1 [.   ]

Month 2 [.   ]

Month 3 [.   ]

Total liability for quarter [.   ] Total must equal line 10.

☐ You were a semiweekly schedule depositor for any part of this quarter. Fill out *Schedule B (Form 941): Report of Tax Liability for Semiweekly Schedule Depositors*, and attach it to this form.

Part 3: Tell us about your business. If a question does NOT apply to your business, leave it blank.

16 If your business has closed or you stopped paying wages . . . . ☐ Check here, and

enter the final date you paid wages [/   /   ] .

17 If you are a seasonal employer and you do not have to file a return for every quarter of the year . . ☐ Check here.

Part 4: May we speak with your third-party designee?

Do you want to allow an employee, a paid tax preparer, or another person to discuss this return with the IRS? See the instructions for details.

☐ Yes. Designee's name [   ]

Phone (___) ___ – ___   Personal Identification Number (PIN) ☐ ☐ ☐ ☐ ☐

☐ No.

Part 5: Sign here. You MUST fill out both sides of this form and SIGN it.

Under penalties of perjury, I declare that I have examined this return, including accompanying schedules and statements, and to the best of my knowledge and belief, it is true, correct, and complete.

X

Sign your name here [   ]

Print name and title [   ]

Date [/   /   ]   Phone (___) ___ – ___

Part 6: For PAID preparers only (optional)

Paid Preparer's Signature [   ]

Firm's name [   ]

Address [   ]   EIN [   ]

[   ]   ZIP code [   ]

Date [/   /   ]   Phone (___) ___ – ___   SSN/PTIN [   ]

☐ Check if you are self-employed.

PROBLEM 8A-4 OR PROBLEM 8B-4

PROBLEM 8A-3 OR PROBLEM 8B-3

Form **941 for 200X:** Employer's QUARTERLY Federal Tax Return   990106
(Rev. January 2006)   Department of the Treasury — Internal Revenue Service
    OMB No. 1545-0029

(EIN)
Employer identification number ☐☐ – ☐☐☐☐☐☐☐

Name *(not your trade name)*

Trade name *(if any)*

Address _____
Number   Street   Suite or room number

City   State   ZIP code

Report for this Quarter ...
(Check one.)

☐ **1:** January, February, March

☐ **2:** April, May, June

☐ **3:** July, August, September

☒ **4:** October, November, December

Read the separate instructions before you fill out this form. Please type or print within the boxes.

Part 1: Answer these questions for this quarter.

1 Number of employees who received wages, tips, or other compensation for the pay period including: *Mar. 12* (Quarter 1), *June 12* (Quarter 2), *Sept. 12* (Quarter 3), *Dec. 12* (Quarter 4) **1** | 3

2 Wages, tips, and other compensation . . . . **2** | 195200.—

3 Total income tax withheld from wages, tips, and other compensation . . . . **3** | 5167.—

4 If no wages, tips, and other compensation are subject to social security or Medicare tax . . ☐ Check and go to line 6.

5 Taxable social security and Medicare wages and tips:

	Column 1		Column 2
5a Taxable social security wages	100970.—	× .124 =	12520.28
5b Taxable social security tips	.	× .124 =	.
5c Taxable Medicare wages & tips	195200.—	× .029 =	5660.80

5d Total social security and Medicare taxes (*Column 2,* lines 5a + 5b + 5c = line 5d) . . **5d** | 18181.08

6 Total taxes before adjustments (lines 3 + 5d = line 6) . . . . **6** | 23348.00

7 **TAX ADJUSTMENTS** (Read the instructions for line 7 before completing lines 7a through 7h.):

7a Current quarter's fractions of cents . . . . | .

7b Current quarter's sick pay . . . . | .

7c Current quarter's adjustments for tips and group-term life insurance | .

7d Current year's income tax withholding (attach Form 941c) . . . | .

7e Prior quarters' social security and Medicare taxes (attach Form 941c) | .

7f Special additions to federal income tax (attach Form 941c) . . . | .

7g Special additions to social security and Medicare (attach Form 941c) | .

7h **TOTAL ADJUSTMENTS** (Combine all amounts: lines 7a through 7g.) . . . . . . **7h** | .

8 Total taxes after adjustments (Combine lines 6 and 7h.) . . . . **8** | .

9 Advance earned income credit (EIC) payments made to employees . . . . . . **9** | .

10 Total taxes after adjustment for advance EIC (line 8 – line 9 = line 10) . . . . . **10** | .

11 Total deposits for this quarter, including overpayment applied from a prior quarter . . **11** | .

12 **Balance due** (If line 10 is more than line 11, write the difference here.) . . . . . . **12** | .
Make checks payable to *United States Treasury.*

13 **Overpayment** (If line 11 is more than line 10, write the difference here.) | . Check one ☐ Apply to next return.
    ☐ Send a refund.

▶ You **MUST** fill out both pages of this form and **SIGN** it.   Next ➡

For Privacy Act and Paperwork Reduction Act Notice, see the back of the Payment Voucher.   Cat. No. 17001Z   Form **941** (Rev. 1-2006)

PROBLEM 8A-4 OR PROBLEM 8B-4

990206

Name *(not your trade name)* | **Employer identification number (EIN)**

Part 2: Tell us about your deposit schedule and tax liability for this quarter.

If you are unsure about whether you are a monthly schedule depositor or a semiweekly schedule depositor, see *Pub. 15 (Circular E)*, section 11.

14 ☐☐ Write the state abbreviation for the state where you made your deposits OR write "MU" if you made your deposits in *multiple* states.

15 Check one: ☐ **Line 10 is less than $2,500.** Go to Part 3.

☐ **You were a monthly schedule depositor for the entire quarter.** Fill out your tax liability for each month. Then go to Part 3.

Tax liability: Month 1 [.]

Month 2 [.]

Month 3 [.]

Total liability for quarter [.] Total must equal line 10.

☐ **You were a semiweekly schedule depositor for any part of this quarter.** Fill out *Schedule B (Form 941): Report of Tax Liability for Semiweekly Schedule Depositors,* and attach it to this form.

Part 3: Tell us about your business. If a question does NOT apply to your business, leave it blank.

16 If your business has closed or you stopped paying wages . . . . ☐ Check here, and

enter the final date you paid wages [/ /] .

17 If you are a seasonal employer and you do not have to file a return for every quarter of the year . . ☐ Check here.

Part 4: May we speak with your third-party designee?

Do you want to allow an employee, a paid tax preparer, or another person to discuss this return with the IRS? See the instructions for details.

☐ Yes. Designee's name [ ]

Phone ( ) – Personal Identification Number (PIN) ☐☐☐☐☐

☐ No.

Part 5: Sign here. You MUST fill out both sides of this form and SIGN it.

Under penalties of perjury, I declare that I have examined this return, including accompanying schedules and statements, and to the best of my knowledge and belief, it is true, correct, and complete.

X Sign your name here [ ]

Print name and title [ ]

Date [/ /] Phone ( ) –

Part 6: For PAID preparers only *(optional)*

Paid Preparer's Signature [ ]

Firm's name [ ]

Address [ ] | EIN [ ]

[ ] | ZIP code [ ]

Date [/ /] Phone ( ) – SSN/PTIN [ ]

☐ Check if you are self-employed.

PROBLEM 8A-5 OR PROBLEM 8B-5

Form **940-EZ**		**Employer's Annual Federal Unemployment (FUTA) Tax Return**	OMB No. 1545-1110
Department of the Treasury Internal Revenue Service		▶ See the separate Instructions for Form 940-EZ for information on completing this form.	**200X**

			T	
You must complete this section. ▶	Name (as distinguished from trade name)	Calendar year	FF	
			FD	
	Trade name, if any	Employer identification number (EIN)	FP	
			I	
	Address (number and street)	City, state, and ZIP code	T	

*Answer the questions under **Who May Use Form 940-EZ** on page 2. If you cannot use Form 940-EZ, you must use Form 940.*

A   Enter the amount of contributions paid to your state unemployment fund (see the separate instructions)   . . ▶ $ ------------------------

B   (1) Enter the name of the state where you have to pay contributions . . . . ▶   ------------------------
      (2) Enter your state reporting number as shown on your state unemployment tax return. ▶

If you will not have to file returns in the future, check here (see **Who Must File** in separate instructions) **and complete and sign the return.** ▶ ☐

If this is an **Amended Return, check here** (see **Amended Returns** in the separate instructions) . . . . ▶ ☐

Part I   **Taxable Wages and FUTA Tax**

1	Total payments (including payments shown on lines 2 and 3) during the calendar year for services of employees	1	
2	Exempt payments. (Explain all exempt payments, attaching additional sheets if necessary.) ▶ ------------------------ ------------------------	2	
3	Payments of more than $7,000 for services. Enter only amounts over the first $7,000 paid to each employee **(see the separate instructions)**	3	
4	Add lines 2 and 3	4	
5	**Total taxable wages** (subtract line 4 from line 1) . . . . . . ▶	5	
6	**FUTA tax.** Multiply the wages on line 5 by .008 and enter here. **(If the result is over $500, also complete Part II.)**	6	
7	Total FUTA tax deposited for the year, including any overpayment applied from a prior year	7	
8	**Balance due** (subtract line 7 from line 6). Pay to the "United States Treasury." . . . . ▶	8	
	If you owe more than $500, see **Depositing FUTA tax** in the separate instructions.		
9	**Overpayment** (subtract line 6 from line 7). Check if it is to be: ☐ **Applied to next return** or ☐ **Refunded** ▶	9	

Part II   **Record of Quarterly Federal Unemployment Tax Liability** (Do not include state liability.) **Complete only if line 6 is over $500.**

Quarter	First (Jan. 1 – Mar. 31)	Second (Apr. 1 – June 30)	Third (July 1 – Sept. 30)	Fourth (Oct. 1 – Dec. 31)	Total for year
Liability for quarter					

Third– Party Designee	Do you want to allow another person to discuss this return with the IRS (see the separate instructions)? ☐ **Yes.** Complete the following. ☐ **No**		
	Designee's name ▶	Phone no. ▶ ( )	Personal identification number (PIN) ▶ ☐☐☐☐☐

Under penalties of perjury, I declare that I have examined this return, including accompanying schedules and statements, and, to the best of my knowledge and belief, it is true, correct, and complete, and that no part of any payment made to a state unemployment fund claimed as a credit was, or is to be, deducted from the payments to employees.

CHAPTER 8
SUMMARY PRACTICE TEST:
THE EMPLOYER'S TAX RESPONSIBILITIES—
PRINCIPLES AND PROCEDURES

Part I Instructions

Fill in the blank(s) to complete the statement.

1. Only the _____ completes the SS-4 Form.
2. The payroll tax expense for the employer is made up of _____, _____, and FUTA.
3. Date from the _____ _____ will provide the needed information to record the payroll in the general journal.
4. SUTA is usually paid _____.
5. FUTA Payable is a _____ found on the _____ _____.
6. Form 941 summarizes the taxes owed for _____ and _____.
7. _____ _____ _____ will tell if a deposit is to be made monthly, or semi-weekly for FIT and Social Security.
8. Form _____ is prepared quarterly to summarize tax liabilities for FICA (Social Security and Medicare) and FIT
9. The _____ _____ _____ _____ is required to be given to employees by January 31 following the year employed.
10. Form 940EZ records the amount of tax liability for _____.

Part II Instructions

Answer true or false to the following.

1. Prepaid Workers' Compensation Insurance is an asset.
2. Workers' compensation need not be estimated at the beginning of the year.
3. Payroll Tax Expense is made up of FICA, SUTA, and FIT
4. Frequency of deposits relating to Form 941 is based on amount of tax liability in lookback periods.
5. The normal balance of FIT payable is a debit.
6. The individual earnings record provides the data to prepare W-2's.
7. A tax calendar provides little help to the employer involving the payment of tax liabilities.
8. Form 941 is completed twice a year.
9. A year-end adjusting entry is needed for workers' compensation.
10. Form 8109 relates only to Form 940EZ.

Part III Instructions

Complete the following table:

ACCOUNT	CATEGORY	FOUND ON WHICH REPORT
1. Payroll Tax Expense		
2. FUTA Payable		
3. SUTA Payable		
4. FICA Tax Payable—Medicare		
5. FIT Payable		
6. Office Salaries Expense		

Part IV Instructions

Complete the following table:

	4 QUARTERS LOOK-BACK PERIOD LIABILITY	PAYROLL PAID WEEKLY	TAX PAID BY:
Sit. A	$40,000	October	?
Sit. B	75,000		
		on Wed.	?
		on Thurs.	?
		on Fri	?
		on Sat.	?
		on Sun.	?
		on Mon.	?
		on. Tues.	?

Why is the depositor in Situation A classified as a Monthly Depositor while in Situation B Depositor is classified as Semi-Weekly?

SOLUTIONS TO SUMMARY PRACTICE TEST

Part I

1. Employer
2. FICA (OASDI and Medicare), SUTA
3. Payroll register
4. quarterly
5. liability, balance sheet
6. FICA (OASDI and Medicare), FIT
7. Look back Periods
8. 941
9. Wage and Tax Statement
10. FUTA

Part II

1. true
2. false
3. false
4. true
5. false

6. true
7. false
8. false
9. true
10. false

Part III

1. Expense; Income Statement
2. Liability; Balance Sheet
3. Liability; Balance Sheet
4. Liability; Balance Sheet
5. Liability; Balance Sheet
6. Expense; Income Statement

Part IV

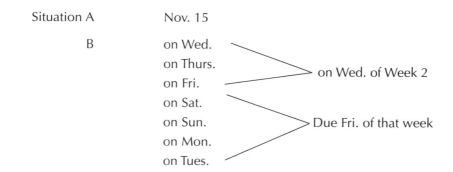

The depositor in situation A is classified as a monthly depositor because their tax liability of $40,000 during the look back period was less than the $50,000 limit.

On the other hand, the depositor in situation B owed $75,000 during the look back period. Since this is greater than the $50,000 limit, they were classified as a semiweekly depositor.

CONTINUING PROBLEM FOR CHAPTER 8
SANCHEZ COMPUTER CENTER

SANCHEZ COMPUTER CENTER
GENERAL JOURNAL

PAGE 9

Date	Account Titles and Description	PR	Dr.	Cr.

CONTINUING PROBLEM

Form **941 for 200X:** **Employer's QUARTERLY Federal Tax Return**

(Rev. January 2006)

Department of the Treasury — Internal Revenue Service

990106

OMB No. 1545-0029

(EIN)
Employer identification number ☐☐ – ☐☐☐☐☐☐☐

Name *(not your trade name)*

Trade name *(if any)*

Address

Number   Street   Suite or room number

City   State   ZIP code

Report for this Quarter ...
(Check one.)

☐ **1:** January, February, March

☐ **2:** April, May, June

☐ **3:** July, August, September

☐ **4:** October, November, December

Read the separate instructions before you fill out this form. Please type or print within the boxes.

Part 1: Answer these questions for this quarter.

1 Number of employees who received wages, tips, or other compensation for the pay period including: *Mar. 12* (Quarter 1), *June 12* (Quarter 2), *Sept. 12* (Quarter 3), *Dec. 12* (Quarter 4)   **1** ▢

2 Wages, tips, and other compensation . . . .   **2** ▢

3 Total income tax withheld from wages, tips, and other compensation . . . .   **3** ▢

4 If no wages, tips, and other compensation are subject to social security or Medicare tax . .   ☐ Check and go to line 6.

5 Taxable social security and Medicare wages and tips:

	Column 1		Column 2
5a Taxable social security wages	▢	× .124 =	▢
5b Taxable social security tips	▢	× .124 =	▢
5c Taxable Medicare wages & tips	▢	× .029 =	▢

5d Total social security and Medicare taxes (*Column 2,* lines 5a + 5b + 5c = line 5d) . **5d** ▢

6 Total taxes before adjustments (lines 3 + 5d = line 6) . . . .   **6** ▢

7 **TAX ADJUSTMENTS** (Read the instructions for line 7 before completing lines 7a through 7h.):

7a Current quarter's fractions of cents . . . .   ▢

7b Current quarter's sick pay . . . .   ▢

7c Current quarter's adjustments for tips and group-term life insurance   ▢

7d Current year's income tax withholding (attach Form 941c) . . .   ▢

7e Prior quarters' social security and Medicare taxes (attach Form 941c)   ▢

7f Special additions to federal income tax (attach Form 941c) . . .   ▢

7g Special additions to social security and Medicare (attach Form 941c)   ▢

7h **TOTAL ADJUSTMENTS** (Combine all amounts: lines 7a through 7g.) . . . . .   **7h** ▢

8 Total taxes after adjustments (Combine lines 6 and 7h.) . . . . . .   **8** ▢

9 Advance earned income credit (EIC) payments made to employees . . . .   **9** ▢

10 Total taxes after adjustment for advance EIC (line 8 – line 9 = line 10) . . . . . .   **10** ▢

11 Total deposits for this quarter, including overpayment applied from a prior quarter . .   **11** ▢

12 **Balance due** (If line 10 is more than line 11, write the difference here.) . . . . . .   **12** ▢
    Make checks payable to *United States Treasury.*

13 **Overpayment** (If line 11 is more than line 10, write the difference here.) ▢   Check one ☐ Apply to next return.
                                                                            ☐ Send a refund.

▶ You **MUST** fill out both pages of this form and **SIGN** it.

Next ➡

For Privacy Act and Paperwork Reduction Act Notice, see the back of the Payment Voucher.   Cat. No. 17001Z   Form **941** (Rev. 1-2006)

CONTINUING PROBLEM

990206

Name *(not your trade name)*	Employer identification number (EIN)

Part 2: Tell us about your deposit schedule and tax liability for this quarter.

If you are unsure about whether you are a monthly schedule depositor or a semiweekly schedule depositor, see *Pub. 15 (Circular E),* section 11.

14 ☐ ☐   Write the state abbreviation for the state where you made your deposits OR write "MU" if you made your deposits in *multiple* states.

15   Check one: ☐   Line 10 is less than $2,500. Go to Part 3.

☐   You were a monthly schedule depositor for the entire quarter. Fill out your tax liability for each month. Then go to Part 3.

Tax liability: Month 1   ☐ .

Month 2   ☐ .

Month 3   ☐ .

Total liability for quarter   ☐ .   Total must equal line 10.

☐   You were a semiweekly schedule depositor for any part of this quarter. Fill out *Schedule B (Form 941): Report of Tax Liability for Semiweekly Schedule Depositors,* and attach it to this form.

Part 3: Tell us about your business. If a question does NOT apply to your business, leave it blank.

16   If your business has closed or you stopped paying wages . . . .   ☐ Check here, and

enter the final date you paid wages   ☐ / / .

17   If you are a seasonal employer and you do not have to file a return for every quarter of the year .   ☐ Check here.

Part 4: May we speak with your third-party designee?

Do you want to allow an employee, a paid tax preparer, or another person to discuss this return with the IRS? See the instructions for details.

☐ Yes. Designee's name ☐

Phone ( ) –   Personal Identification Number (PIN) ☐ ☐ ☐ ☐ ☐

☐ No.

Part 5: Sign here. You MUST fill out both sides of this form and SIGN it.

Under penalties of perjury, I declare that I have examined this return, including accompanying schedules and statements, and to the best of my knowledge and belief, it is true, correct, and complete.

✗   Sign your name here ☐

Print name and title ☐

Date ☐ / /   Phone ( ) –

Part 6: For PAID preparers only *(optional)*

Paid Preparer's Signature		
Firm's name		
Address		EIN
		ZIP code
Date / / Phone ( ) –		SSN/PTIN

☐ Check if you are self-employed.

CONTINUING PROBLEM

Form **940-EZ**	**Employer's Annual Federal Unemployment (FUTA) Tax Return**	OMB No. 1545-1110
Department of the Treasury Internal Revenue Service	▶ **See the separate Instructions for Form 940-EZ for information on completing this form.**	**200X**

	Name (as distinguished from trade name)	Calendar year		T
You must complete this section. ▶				FF
				FD
	Trade name, if any	Employer identification number (EIN)		FP
				I
	Address (number and street)	City, state, and ZIP code		T

*Answer the questions under **Who May Use Form 940-EZ** on page 2. If you cannot use Form 940-EZ, you must use Form 940.*

A Enter the amount of contributions paid to your state unemployment fund (see the separate instructions) . . ▶ $ _____

B (1) Enter the name of the state where you have to pay contributions . . . . ▶ _____

   (2) Enter your state reporting number as shown on your state unemployment tax return. ▶ _____

If you will not have to file returns in the future, check here (see **Who Must File** in separate instructions) **and complete and sign the return.** ▶ ☐

If this is an Amended Return, check here (see **Amended Returns** in the separate instructions) . . . . ▶ ☐

Part I	**Taxable Wages and FUTA Tax**		
1	Total payments (including payments shown on lines 2 and 3) during the calendar year for services of employees	**1**	
2	Exempt payments. (Explain all exempt payments, attaching additional sheets if necessary.) ▶ _____ _____	**2**	
3	Payments of more than $7,000 for services. Enter only amounts over the first $7,000 paid to each employee (see the separate instructions)	**3**	
4	Add lines 2 and 3	**4**	
5	**Total taxable wages** (subtract line 4 from line 1) . . . . ▶	**5**	
6	**FUTA tax.** Multiply the wages on line 5 by .008 and enter here. **(If the result is over $500, also complete Part II.)**	**6**	
7	Total FUTA tax deposited for the year, including any overpayment applied from a prior year	**7**	
8	**Balance due** (subtract line 7 from line 6). Pay to the "United States Treasury." . . . . ▶	**8**	
	If you owe more than $500, see **Depositing FUTA tax** in the separate instructions.		
9	**Overpayment** (subtract line 6 from line 7). Check if it is to be: ☐ **Applied to next return** or ☐ **Refunded** ▶	**9**	

Part II	**Record of Quarterly Federal Unemployment Tax Liability** (Do not include state liability.) **Complete only if line 6 is over $500.**				
Quarter	First (Jan. 1 – Mar. 31)	Second (Apr. 1 – June 30)	Third (July 1 – Sept. 30)	Fourth (Oct. 1 – Dec. 31)	Total for year
Liability for quarter					

Third–Party Designee	Do you want to allow another person to discuss this return with the IRS (see the separate instructions)? ☐ **Yes.** Complete the following. ☐ **No**		
	Designee's name ▶	Phone no. ▶ ( )	Personal identification number (PIN) ▶ ☐☐☐☐☐

Under penalties of perjury, I declare that I have examined this return, including accompanying schedules and statements, and, to the best of my knowledge and belief, it is true, correct, and complete, and that no part of any payment made to a state unemployment fund claimed as a credit was, or is to be, deducted from the payments to employees.

SALES AND CASH RECEIPTS

9

SELF-REVIEW QUIZ 9-1

1. _____   2. _____   3. _____   4. _____   5. _____

SELF-REVIEW QUIZ 9-2   **BERNIE COMPANY**
                             GENERAL JOURNAL

PAGE 1

Date	Account Titles and Description	PR	Dr.	Cr.

ACCOUNTS RECEIVABLE SUBSIDIARY LEDGER

NAME   LEE CORP.

ADDRESS   118 MORRIS RD., BOSTON, MA 01935

Date	Explanation	Post Ref.	Debit	Credit	Dr. Balance

NAME   RING COMPANY

ADDRESS   31 NORRIS ROAD, BOSTON MA 01935

Date	Explanation	Post Ref.	Debit	Credit	Dr. Balance

PARTIAL GENERAL LEDGER

ACCOUNT RECEIVABLE   **ACCOUNT NO. 141**

Date	Explanation	Post Ref.	Debit	Credit	Balance	
					Debit	Credit

SALES   **ACCOUNT NO. 310**

Date	Explanation	Post Ref.	Debit	Credit	Balance	
					Debit	Credit

SALES RETURNS AND ALLOWANCES   **ACCOUNT NO. 312**

Date	Explanation	Post Ref.	Debit	Credit	Balance	
					Debit	Credit

SELF-REVIEW QUIZ 9-3

MABEL CORPORATION
GENERAL JOURNAL

PAGE 3

Date	Account Titles and Description	PR	Dr.	Cr.

PARTIAL GENERAL LEDGER

CASH   ACCOUNT NO. 110

Date 200X		Explanation	Post Ref.	Debit	Credit	Balance Debit	Balance Credit
May	1	Balance	✔			6 0 0 00	

ACCOUNTS RECEIVABLE   ACCOUNT NO. 120

Date 200X		Explanation	Post Ref.	Debit	Credit	Balance Debit	Balance Credit
May	1	Balance	✔			7 0 0 00	

STORE EQUIPMENT   ACCOUNT NO. 130

Date 200X		Explanation	Post Ref.	Debit	Credit	Balance Debit	Balance Credit
May	1	Balance	✔			6 0 0 00	

SALES   ACCOUNT NO. 410

Date 200X		Explanation	Post Ref.	Debit	Credit	Balance Debit	Balance Credit
May	1	Balance	✔				7 0 0 00

SALES DISCOUNT   ACCOUNT NO. <u>420</u>

Date 200X		Explanation	Post Ref.	Debit	Credit	Balance	
						Debit	Credit

NAME JANIS FROSS

ADDRESS 81 FOSTER RD., BEVERLY, MA 09125

Date 200X		Explanation	Post Ref.	Debit	Credit	Dr. Balance
May	1	Balance	✔			2 0 0 00

ACCOUNTS RECEIVABLE SUBSIDIARY LEDGER

NAME IRENE WELCH

ADDRESS 10 RONG RD., BEVERLY, MA 01215

Date 200X		Explanation	Post Ref.	Debit	Credit	Dr. Balance
May	1	Balance	✔			5 0 0 00

CHAPTER 9
FORMS FOR CLASSROOM DEMONSTRATION EXERCISES SET A OR SET B

1.

2.

3.

A. _____   _____
B. _____   _____
C. _____   _____

4.

5.

Date		Account Titles and Description	PR		Dr.		Cr.

6.

BLUE CO.
SCHEDULE OF ACCOUNTS RECEIVABLE
MAY 31, 200X

FORMS FOR EXERCISES

9-1.

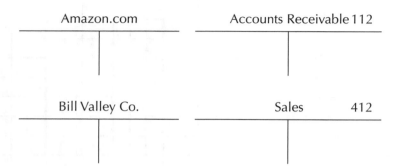

Amazon.com	Accounts Receivable 112

Bill Valley Co.	Sales 412

9-2.

GENERAL JOURNAL

PAGE 1

Date	Account Titles and Description	PR	Dr.	Cr.

Bass Co.	Sales 411

Ronald Co.	Accounts Receivable 112	Sales Returns & Allowances 412

EXERCISES (CONTINUED)

9-3.

9-4.

EDNA CO.
GENERAL JOURNAL

PAGE 1

Date	Account Titles and Description	PR	Dr.	Cr.

EXERCISES (CONTINUED)

GENERAL JOURNAL

PAGE 1

Date	Account Titles and Description	PR	Dr.	Cr.

ACCOUNTS RECEIVABLE SUBSIDIARY LEDGER

Boston Co.

Gary Co.

PARTIAL GENERAL LEDGER

Cash   111

Accounts Receivable   113

Edna Cares, Capital   311

Sales   411

Sales Returns &
Allowances   412

Sales Discount   413

EDNA CO.
SCHEDULE OF ACCOUNTS RECEIVABLE
JUNE 30, 200X

9-5.

END OF CHAPTER PROBLEMS

PROBLEM 9A-1 OR PROBLEM 9B-1

FOOD ON THE GO
GENERAL JOURNAL

PAGE 1

Date	Account Titles and Description	PR	Dr.	Cr.

PROBLEM 9A-1 OR PROBLEM 9B-1 (CONTINUED)

ACCOUNTS RECEIVABLE SUBSIDIARY LEDGER

NAME DUNCAN CO.

ADDRESS 942 MOSE ST., REVERE. MA 01938

Date	Explanation	Post Ref.	Debit	Credit	Dr. Balance

NAME LONG CO.

ADDRESS 8 JOSS AVE., LYNN, MA 01947

Date	Explanation	Post Ref.	Debit	Credit	Dr. Balance

NAME SUE MOORE CO.

ADDRESS 10 LOST RD., TOPSFIELD, MA 01998

Date	Explanation	Post Ref.	Debit	Credit	Dr. Balance

PROBLEM 9A-1 OR PROBLEM 9B-1 (CONTINUED)

FOOD ON THE GO
GENERAL LEDGER

ACCOUNTS RECEIVABLE   **ACCOUNT NO. 112**

Date		Explanation	Post Ref.	Debit	Credit	Balance	
						Debit	Credit

PIZZA SALES   **ACCOUNT NO. 410**

Date		Explanation	Post Ref.	Debit	Credit	Balance	
						Debit	Credit

GROCERY SALES   **ACCOUNT NO. 411**

Date		Explanation	Post Ref.	Debit	Credit	Balance	
						Debit	Credit

SALES RETURNS AND ALLOWANCES   **ACCOUNT NO. 412**

Date		Explanation	Post Ref.	Debit	Credit	Balance	
						Debit	Credit

PROBLEM 9A-1 OR PROBLEM 9B-1 (CONCLUDED)

FOOD ON THE GO
SCHEDULE OF ACCOUNTS RECEIVABLE
JUNE 30, 200X

PROBLEM 9A-2 OR PROBLEM 9B-2

TED'S AUTO SUPPLY
GENERAL JOURNAL

PAGE 2

Date	Account Titles and Description	PR	Dr.	Cr.

PROBLEM 9A-2 OR PROBLEM 9B-2

ACCOUNTS RECEIVABLE SUBSIDIARY LEDGER

NAME   LANCE CORNER

ADDRESS   9 ROE ST., BARTLETT, NH 01382

Date 200X		Explanation	Post Ref.	Debit	Credit	Dr. Balance
NOV	1	Balance	✔			4 0 0 00

NAME   J. SETH

ADDRESS   22 REESE ST., LACONIA, NH 04321

Date 200X		Explanation	Post Ref.	Debit	Credit	Dr. Balance
NOV	1	Balance	✔			2 0 0 00

NAME   R. VOLAN

ADDRESS   12 ASTER RD., MERIMACK, NH 02134

Date 200X		Explanation	Post Ref.	Debit	Credit	Dr. Balance
NOV	1	Balance	✔			1 0 0 0 00

PROBLEM 9A-2 OR PROBLEM 9B-2 (CONTINUED)

TED'S AUTO SUPPLY
PARTIAL GENERAL LEDGER

ACCOUNTS RECEIVABLE **ACCOUNT NO. 110**

Date 200X	Explanation	Post Ref.	Debit	Credit	Balance Debit	Balance Credit
NOV 1	Balance	✔			1 6 0 0 00	

SALES TAX PAYABLE **ACCOUNT NO. 210**

Date 200X	Explanation	Post Ref.	Debit	Credit	Balance Debit	Balance Credit
NOV 1	Balance	✔				1 6 0 0 00

AUTO PARTS SALES **ACCOUNT NO. 410**

Date	Explanation	Post Ref.	Debit	Credit	Balance Debit	Balance Credit

SALES RETURNS AND ALLOWANCES **ACCOUNT NO. 420**

Date	Explanation	Post Ref.	Debit	Credit	Balance Debit	Balance Credit

PROBLEM 9A-2 OR PROBLEM 9B-2 (CONCLUDED)

(3)

TED'S AUTO SUPPLY
SCHEDULE OF ACCOUNTS RECEIVABLE
NOVEMBER 30, 200X

PROBLEM 9A-3 OR PROBLEM 9B-3
(1,2)

PEAKER'S SNEAKER SHOP
GENERAL JOURNAL

PAGE 2

Date	Account Titles and Description	PR	Dr.	Cr.

PROBLEM 9A-3 OR PROBLEM 9B-3 (CONTINUED)

(1,2)

PEAKER'S SNEAKER SHOP
GENERAL JOURNAL

PAGE 3

Date	Account Titles and Description	PR	Dr.	Cr.

PROBLEM 9A-3 OR PROBLEM 9B-3 (CONTINUED)

ACCOUNTS RECEIVABLE SUBSIDIARY LEDGER

NAME B. DALE

ADDRESS 1822 RIVER RD., MEMPHIS, TN 09111

Date 200X		Explanation	Post Ref.	Debit	Credit	Dr. Balance
MAY	1	Balance	✔			4 0 0 00

NAME RON LESTER

ADDRESS 18 MASS. AVE., SAN DIEGO, CA 01999

Date		Explanation	Post Ref.	Debit	Credit	Dr. Balance
MAY	1	Balance	✔			8 0 0 00

PROBLEM 9A-3 OR PROBLEM 9B-3 (CONTINUED)

ACCOUNTS RECEIVABLE SUBSIDIARY LEDGER

NAME   PAM PRY

ADDRESS   918 MOORE DR., HOMEWOOD, IL 60430

Date 200X		Explanation	Post Ref.	Debit	Credit	Dr. Balance
MAY	1	Balance	✔			6 0 0 00

NAME   JIM ZON

ADDRESS   2 CHESTNUT ST., SWAMPSCOTT, MA 01970

Date 200X		Explanation	Post Ref.	Debit	Credit	Dr. Balance
MAY	1	Balance	✔			4 0 0 00

PEAKER'S SNEAKER SHOP
PARTIAL GENERAL LEDGER

CASH **ACCOUNT NO. 10**

Date 200X		Explanation	Post Ref.	Debit	Credit	Balance Debit	Balance Credit
MAY	1	Balance	✔			15 5 0 0 00	

PROBLEM 9A-3 OR PROBLEM 9B-3 (CONTINUED)

ACCOUNTS RECEIVABLE ACCOUNT NO. 12

Date 200X	Explanation	Post Ref.	Debit	Credit	Balance Debit	Balance Credit
MAY 1	Balance	✔			2 2 0 0 00	

SNEAKER RACK EQUIPMENT ACCOUNT NO. 14

Date 200X	Explanation	Post Ref.	Debit	Credit	Balance Debit	Balance Credit
MAY 1	Balance	✔			1 0 0 0 00	

MARK PEAKER, CAPITAL ACCOUNT NO. 30

Date 200X	Explanation	Post Ref.	Debit	Credit	Balance Debit	Balance Credit
MAY 1	Balance	✔				40 0 0 0 00

SALES   **ACCOUNT NO. 40**

Date 200X	Explanation	Post Ref.	Debit	Credit	Balance Debit	Balance Credit
MAY 1	Balance	✔				2 2 0 0 00

SALES DISCOUNT   **ACCOUNT NO. 42**

Date 200X	Explanation	Post Ref.	Debit	Credit	Balance Debit	Balance Credit

SALES RETURNS & ALLOWANCES   **ACCOUNT NO. 44**

Date 200X	Explanation	Post Ref.	Debit	Credit	Balance Debit	Balance Credit

PEAKER'S SNEAKER SHOP
SCHEDULE OF ACCOUNTS RECEIVABLE
MAY 31, 200X

PROBLEM 9A-4 OR PROBLEM 9B-4

BILL'S COSMETIC MARKET
GENERAL JOURNAL

PAGE 1

Date	Account Titles and Description	PR	Dr.	Cr.

PROBLEM 9A-4 OR PROBLEM 9B-4 (CONTINUED)

BILL'S COSMETIC MARKET
GENERAL JOURNAL

Date		Account Titles and Description	PR	Dr.	Cr.

PROBLEM 9A-4 OR PROBLEM 9B-4 (CONTINUED)

ACCOUNTS RECEIVABLE SUBSIDIARY LEDGER

NAME   ALICE KOY CO.

ADDRESS   2 RYAN RD., BUFFALO, NY 09113

Date	Explanation	Post Ref.	Debit	Credit	Debit Balance

PROBLEM 9A-4 OR PROBLEM 9B-4 (CONTINUED)

ACCOUNTS RECEIVABLE SUBSIDIARY LEDGER

NAME RUSTY NEAL CO.

ADDRESS 4 REEL RD., LANCASTER, PA 04332

Date	Explanation	Post Ref.	Debit	Credit	Debit Balance

NAME MARIKA SANCHEZ CO.

ADDRESS 14 BONE DR., ENGLEWOOD CLIFFS, NJ 07632

Date	Explanation	Post Ref.	Debit	Credit	Debit Balance

NAME JEFF TONG CO.

ADDRESS 2 MARION RD., BOSTON, MA 01981

Date	Explanation	Post Ref.	Debit	Credit	Debit Balance

PROBLEM 9A-4 OR PROBLEM 9B-4 (CONTINUED)

BILL'S COSMETIC MARKET
GENERAL LEDGER

CASH   ACCOUNT NO. 10

Date	Explanation	Post Ref.	Debit	Credit	Balance Debit	Balance Credit

ACCOUNTS RECEIVABLE   ACCOUNT NO. 12

Date	Explanation	Post Ref.	Debit	Credit	Balance Debit	Balance Credit

PROBLEM 9A-4 OR PROBLEM 9B-4 (CONTINUED)

SALES TAX PAYABLE   ACCOUNT NO. 20

Date		Explanation	Post Ref.	Debit	Credit	Balance	
						Debit	Credit

BILL MURRAY, CAPITAL   ACCOUNT NO. 30

Date		Explanation	Post Ref.	Debit	Credit	Balance	
						Debit	Credit

LIPSTICK SALES   ACCOUNT NO. 40

Date		Explanation	Post Ref.	Debit	Credit	Balance	
						Debit	Credit

PROBLEM 9A-4 OR PROBLEM 9B-4 (CONTINUED)

SALES RETURNS & ALLOWANCES, LIPSTICK   ACCOUNT NO. 42

Date	Explanation	Post Ref.	Debit	Credit	Balance Debit	Balance Credit

EYESHADOW SALES   ACCOUNT NO. 44

Date	Explanation	Post Ref.	Debit	Credit	Balance Debit	Balance Credit

PROBLEM 9A-4 (CONCLUDED)

(3)

BILL'S COSMETIC MARKET
SCHEDULE OF ACCOUNTS RECEIVABLE
APRIL 30, 200X

CHAPTER 9
SUMMARY PRACTICE TEST
SALES AND CASH RECEIPTS

Part I Instructions

Fill in the blank(s) to complete the statement.

1. The normal balance of sales discounts is _____.
2. _____ _____ and _____ is a contra-revenue account.
3. Sales discount is a _____ account.
4. A discount period is less time than the _____ _____.
5. A debit to accounts receivable and a credit to sales records the sale of merchandise _____ _____ .
6. The _____ _____ _____ _____ lists in alphabetical order an account for each customer.
7. _____ _____ in the general ledger is called the controlling account.
8. The (✔) in the PR column of the general journal indicates that the accounts receivable ledger has been updated.
9. Issuing _____ _____ results in a debit to sales returns and allowancs and a credit to accounts receivable.
10. In a wholesale company there is no _____ tax.
11. Sales Tax Payable is a _____ in the general ledger.
12. Cash sales result in a _____ to cash and a _____ to sales.
13. Sales Returns and Allowances is a _____ account.
14. The _____ _____ has to be posted to the general as well as the sales ledger.
15. No _____ _____ are taken on sales tax.
16. A _____ _____ _____ lists the ending balances from the accounts receivable ledger.

Part II

Complete to following chart:

Transaction	Dr.	Cr.
1. Sale on account	_____	_____
2. Issued credit memo	_____	_____
3. Cash sale	_____	_____
4. Received cash payment less discount	_____	_____

Partial Chart of Accounts

10 Cash
20 Accounts Receivable

40 Sales
42 Sales Discount
44 Sales Returns and Allowances

Part III Instructions

Answer true or false to the following statements.

1. A schedule of accounts receivable is prepared from the general ledger.
2. A perpetual system would keep continual track of inventory.
3. Sales Discount Policies can never change..
4. Sales Tax Payable is an asset.
5. Sales Discount is a contra asset.
6. Issuing a credit memorandum results in Sales, Returns and Allowances decreasing with Accounts Receivable increasing.
7. The sum of the accounts receivable subsidiary ledger is equal to the balance in the controlling account at the end of the month.
8. The Buyer issues the credit memo.
9. The accounts receivable subsidiary ledger is listed in numerical order.
10. Sales Returns and Allowances is a contra-revenue account.
11. Net sales = gross sales − SRA-SD.
12. The normal balance of an Accounts Receivable Ledger is a debit.
13. Discounts are taken on sales tax.
14. 2110,N/30 means a cash discount is good for 30 days.
15. The accounts receivable subsidiary ledger is always located in the general ledger.
16. Gross profit plus operating expenses equals net income.
17. A credit period is longer than the discount period.
18. In the accounts receivable subsidiary ledger each account is debited to record amounts customers owe.
19. Sales Tax Payable could be part of a credit memo.

CHAPTER 9
SOLUTIONS TO SUMMARY PRACTICE TEST

Part I

1.	Debit	9.	sales
2.	Sales Returns and Allowances	10.	liability
3.	contra-revenue	11.	debit, credit
4.	credit period	12.	contra-revenue
5.	on account	13.	journalized transactions
6.	accounts receivable subsidiary ledger	14.	cash discounts
7.	during the month	15.	schedule of accounts receivable
8.	end of the month		

SOLUTIONS TO SUMMARY PRACTICE TEST

Part II

	Dr.	Cr.
1.	20	40
2.	44	20
3.	10	40
4.	10	20
	42	

Part III

1.	false		**11.**	true
2.	true		**12.**	true
3.	false		**13.**	true
4.	false		**14.**	false
5.	false		**15.**	false
6.	false		**16.**	false
7.	false		**17.**	false
8.	true		**18.**	true
9.	false		**19.**	true
10.	false		**20.**	true

SANCHEZ COMPUTER CENTER
GENERAL JOURNAL

Date	Account Titles and Description	PR	Dr.	Cr.

SANCHEZ COMPUTER CENTER
SCHEDULE OF ACCOUNTS RECEIVABLE
1/31/0X

CASH   **ACCOUNT NO. 1000**

Date		Explanation	Post Ref.	Debit	Credit	Balance Debit	Balance Credit
1/1	0X	Balance Forward	✔			3 3 3 6 65	

SANCHEZ COMPUTER CENTER
PARTIAL GENERAL LEDGER

ACCOUNTS RECEIVABLE   **ACCOUNT NO. 1020**

Date		Explanation	Post Ref.	Debit	Credit	Balance Debit	Balance Credit
1/1	0X	Balance Forward				13 600 00	

SALES   **ACCOUNT NO. 4010**

Date		Explanation	Post Ref.	Debit	Credit	Balance Debit	Balance Credit

SALES RETURN AND ALLOWANCES   **ACCOUNT NO. 4020**

Date		Explanation	Post Ref.	Debit	Credit	Balance Debit	Balance Credit

SALES DISCOUNTS   **ACCOUNT NO. 4030**

Date		Explanation	Post Ref.	Debit	Credit	Balance Debit	Balance Credit

ACCOUNTS RECEIVABLE
SUBSIDIARY LEDGER

NAME   TAYLOR GOLF   **ACCOUNT NO. 100**

ADDRESS   1010 MOCKINGBIRD LANE, CARLSBAD, CA 92008

Date		Explanation	Post Ref.	Debit	Credit	Dr. Balance
1/1	0X	Balance forward	✔			2 9 0 0 00

NAME   VITA NEEDLE   **ACCOUNT NO. 101**

ADDRESS   144 CANTATA, IRVINE, CA 92606

Date		Explanation	Post Ref.	Debit	Credit	Dr. Balance
1/1	0X	Balance	✔			6 8 0 0 00

NAME   ACCUPAC   **ACCOUNT NO. 103**

ADDRESS   1717 JORDAN ST., SAN CLEMENTE, CA 91607

Date		Explanation	Post Ref.	Debit	Credit	Dr. Balance
1/1	0X	Balance	✔			3 9 0 0 00

ACCOUNTS RECEIVABLE SUBSIDIARY LEDGER

NAME ANTHONY J. PITALE   **ACCOUNT NO.** 104

ADDRESS 600 NEWPORT BEACH, NEWPORT, CA 91600

Date		Explanation	Post Ref.	Debit	Credit	Dr. Balance

10

PURCHASES AND CASH PAYMENTS

SELF-REVIEW QUIZ 10-1

1. _____ 2. _____ 3. _____ 4. _____ 5. _____

SELF-REVIEW QUIZ 10-2

MUNROE CO.
GENERAL JOURNAL

PAGE 1

Date	Account Titles and Description	PR	Dr.	Cr.

ACCOUNTS PAYABLE SUBSIDIARY LEDGER

NAME   JOHN BUTLER COMPANY

ADDRESS   18 REED RD., HOMEWOOD, IL 60430

Date	Explanation	Post Ref.	Debit	Credit	Cr. Balance

NAME   FLYNN COMPANY

ADDRESS   15 FOSS AVE., ENGLEWOOD CLIFFS, NJ 07632

Date	Explanation	Post Ref.	Debit	Credit	Cr. Balance

PARTIAL GENERAL LEDGER

EQUIPMENT   **ACCOUNT NO. 121**

Date	Explanation	Post Ref.	Debit	Credit	Balance Debit	Balance Credit

ACCOUNTS PAYABLE   ACCOUNT NO. 212

Date	Explanation	Post Ref.	Debit	Credit	Balance Debit	Balance Credit

PURCHASES   ACCOUNT NO. 512

Date	Explanation	Post Ref.	Debit	Credit	Balance Debit	Balance Credit

PURCHASES RETURNS AND ALLOWANCES   ACCOUNT NO. 513

Date	Explanation	Post Ref.	Debit	Credit	Balance Debit	Balance Credit

SELF REVIEW QUIZ 10-3

MELISSA COMPANY
GENERAL JOURNAL

PAGE 2

Date	Account Titles and Description	PR	Dr.	Cr.

ACCOUNTS PAYABLE SUBSIDARY LEDGER

NAME   BOB FINKELSTEIN

ADDRESS   112 FLYING HIGHWAY, TRENTON, NJ 00861

Date 200X		Explanation	Post Ref.	Debit	Credit	Cr. Balance
June	1	Balance	✔			3 0 0 00

NAME   AL JEEP

ADDRESS   118 WANG RD., SAUGUS, MA 01432

Date 200X		Explanation	Post Ref.	Debit	Credit	Cr. Balance
June	1	Balance	✔			2 0 0 00

PARTIAL GENERAL LEDGER

CASH   ACCOUNT NO. 110

Date 200X		Explanation	Post Ref.	Debit	Credit	Balance Debit	Balance Credit
June	1	Balance	✔			7 0 0 00	

ACCOUNTS PAYABLE   ACCOUNT NO. 210

Date 200X		Explanation	Post Ref.	Debit	Credit	Balance Debit	Balance Credit
June	1	Balance	✔				5 0 0 00

PURCHASES DISCOUNT   ACCOUNT NO. 511

Date		Explanation	Post Ref.	Debit	Credit	Balance Debit	Balance Credit

ADVERTISING EXPENSE   ACCOUNT NO. 610

Date		Explanation	Post Ref.	Debit	Credit	Balance Debit	Balance Credit

SELF REVIEW QUIZ 10-4

PETE'S CLOCK SHOP
GENERAL JOURNAL

Date	Account Titles and Description	PR	Dr.	Cr.

SELF REVIEW QUIZ 10-4

PETE'S CLOCK SHOP
GENERAL JOURNAL

PAGE 3

Date	Account Titles and Description	PR	Dr.	Cr.

CHAPTER 10
FORMS FOR CLASSROOM DEMONSTRATION EXERCISES SET A OR SET B

1. A. _____   D. _____
    B. _____   E. _____
    C. _____   F. _____

2.

3. _____
    _____
    _____
    _____
    _____
    _____
    _____
    _____

4. A. _____
    B. _____
    C. _____

5.

6.

WEB.COM
SCHEDULE OF ACCOUNTS PAYABLE
MAY 31, 200X

FORM FOR CLASSROOM DEMONSTRATION EXERCISES 7, 8, 9, 10

Date		Account Titles and Description	PR	Dr.		Cr.	

FORMS FOR EXERCISES

10-1.

Rey.com	Equipment 120
Lane.com	Accounts Payable 210
Sail.com	Purchases 510

10-2.   PAGE 1

		Purchases Returns and
Reel Co.	Accounts Payable 211	Allowances 513

FORMS FOR EXERCISES (CONTINUED)

10-3.   PAGE 2

Date	Account Titles and Description	PR	Dr.	Cr.

ACCOUNTS PAYABLE SUBSIDIARY LEDGER

A. James
	1,000

B. Foss
	400

J. Ranch
	900

B. Swanson
	100

PARTIAL GENERAL LEDGER

Cash   110
3,000	

Accounts Payable   210
	2,400

Purchases Discount   511

Advertising Expense   610

EXERCISES (CONTINUED)

10-4.

MORGAN'S CLOTHING
SCHEDULE OF ACCOUNTS PAYABLE
APRIL 30, 200X

_____

_____

_____

_____

Accounts Payable   210

10-5.

Accounts Affected	Category	↑↓	Rules

10-6.

_____

_____

_____

_____

_____

_____

FORM FOR EXERCISES 10-7, 10-8, 10-9, 10-10

Date	Account Titles and Description	PR	Dr.	Cr.

CALCULATION PAGE FOR 10-7 TO 10-10

PROBLEM 10A-1 OR PROBLEM 10B-1

BERNIE KRINE
GENERAL JOURNAL

10-1.

Date	Account Titles and Description	PR	Dr.	Cr.

PROBLEM 10A-1 OR PROBLEM 10B-1 (CONTINUED)

ACCOUNTS PAYABLE SUBSIDIARY LEDGER

NAME   MAIL.COM

ADDRESS   12 SMITH ST., DEARBORN, MI 09113

Date		Explanation	Post Ref.	Debit	Credit	Cr. Balance

NAME   NORTON CO.

ADDRESS   1 RANTOUL RD., CHARLOTTE, NC 01114

Date		Explanation	Post Ref.	Debit	Credit	Cr. Balance

NAME   ROLO CO.

ADDRESS   2 WEST RD., LYNN, MA 01471

Date		Explanation	Post Ref.	Debit	Credit	Cr. Balance

PARTIAL GENERAL LEDGER

STORE SUPPLIES   **ACCOUNT NO. 115**

Date		Explanation	Post Ref.	Debit	Credit	Balance	
						Debit	Credit

PROBLEM 10A-1 OR PROBLEM 10B-1 (CONCLUDED)

STORE EQUIPMENT   ACCOUNT NO. 121

Date	Explanation	Post Ref.	Debit	Credit	Balance Debit	Balance Credit

ACCOUNTS PAYABLE   ACCOUNT NO. 210

Date	Explanation	Post Ref.	Debit	Credit	Balance Debit	Balance Credit

PURCHASES   ACCOUNT NO. 510

Date	Explanation	Post Ref.	Debit	Credit	Balance Debit	Balance Credit

PROBLEM 10A-2 OR PROBLEM 10B-2

MABEL'S NATURAL FOODSTORE

PAGE 2

Date	Account Titles and Description	PR	Dr.	Cr.

PROBLEM 10A-2 OR PROBLEM 10B-2 (CONTINUED)

ACCOUNTS PAYABLE SUBSIDIARY LEDGER

NAME   ATON CO.

ADDRESS   11 LYNNWAY AVE., NEWPORT, RI 03112

Date 200X		Explanation	Post Ref.	Debit	Credit	Cr. Balance
MAY	1	Balance	✔			4 0 0 00

NAME   BROWARD CO.

ADDRESS   21 RIVER ST., ANAHEIM, CA 43110

Date 200X		Explanation	Post Ref.	Debit	Credit	Cr. Balance
MAY	1	Balance	✔			6 0 0 00

NAME   MIDDEN CO.

ADDRESS   10 ASTER RD., DUBUQUE, IA 80021

Date 200X		Explanation	Post Ref.	Debit	Credit	Cr. Balance
MAY	1	Balance	✔			1 2 0 0 00

NAME   RELAR CO.

ADDRESS   22 GERALD RD., SMITH, CO 43138

Date 200X		Explanation	Post Ref.	Debit	Credit	Cr. Balance
MAY	1	Balance	✔			5 0 0 00

PROBLEM 10A-2 OR PROBLEM 10B-2 (CONTINUED)

PARTIAL GENERAL LEDGER

STORE SUPPLIES   **ACCOUNT NO. 110**

Date	Explanation	Post Ref.	Debit	Credit	Balance Debit	Balance Credit

OFFICE EQUIPMENT   **ACCOUNT NO. 120**

Date	Explanation	Post Ref.	Debit	Credit	Balance Debit	Balance Credit

ACCOUNTS PAYABLE   **ACCOUNT NO. 210**

Date 200X	Explanation	Post Ref.	Debit	Credit	Balance Debit	Balance Credit
MAY 1	Balance	✔				2 7 0 0 00

PURCHASES   **ACCOUNT NO. 510**

Date 200X	Explanation	Post Ref.	Debit	Credit	Balance Debit	Balance Credit
MAY 1	Balance	✔			16 0 0 0 00	

PROBLEM 10A-2 OR PROBLEM 10B-2 (CONCLUDED)

PURCHASES RETURNS AND ALLOWANCES   ACCOUNT NO. 512

Date	Explanation	Post Ref.	Debit	Credit	Balance	
					Debit	Credit

MABEL'S NATURAL FOOD STORE

SCHEDULE OF ACCOUNTS PAYABLE

MAY 31, 200X

PROBLEM 10A-3 OR PROBLEM 10B-3

PAGE 5

Date		Account Titles and Description	PR		Dr.			Cr.	

PROBLEM 10A-3 OR PROBLEM 10B-3 (CONTINUED)

ACCOUNTS PAYABLE SUBSIDIARY LEDGER

NAME   ALVIN CO.

ADDRESS   1 REACH RD., IPSWICH, MA 01932

Date 200X		Explanation	Post Ref.	Debit	Credit	Cr. Balance
MAY	1	Balance	✔			1 2 0 0 00

NAME   HENRY CO.

ADDRESS   1 RALPH RD., REVERE, MA 01321

Date 200X		Explanation	Post Ref.	Debit	Credit	Cr. Balance
MAY	1	Balance	✔			6 0 0 00

NAME   SOY CO.

ADDRESS   7 PLYMOUTH AVE., GLENN, NH 01218

Date 200X		Explanation	Post Ref.	Debit	Credit	Cr. Balance
MAY	1	Balance	✔			8 0 0 00

NAME   XON CO.

ADDRESS   22 REY RD., BOCA RATON, FL 99132

Date 200X		Explanation	Post Ref.	Debit	Credit	Cr. Balance
MAY	1	Balance	✔			1 4 0 0 00

PROBLEM 10A-3 OR PROBLEM 10B-3 (CONTINUED)

PARTIAL GENERAL LEDGER

CASH ACCOUNT NO. 110

Date 200X		Explanation	Post Ref.	Debit	Credit	Balance Debit	Balance Credit
MAY	1	Balance	✔			17 000 00	

DELIVERY TRUCK ACCOUNT NO. 150

Date 200X		Explanation	Post Ref.	Debit	Credit	Balance Debit	Balance Credit

ACCOUNTS PAYABLE ACCOUNT NO. 210

Date 200X		Explanation	Post Ref.	Debit	Credit	Balance Debit	Balance Credit
MAY	1	Balance	✔				4 000 00

COMPUTER PURCHASES ACCOUNT NO. 510

Date 200X		Explanation	Post Ref.	Debit	Credit	Balance Debit	Balance Credit

PROBLEM 10A-3 OR PROBLEM 10B-3 (CONCLUDED)

COMPUTER PURCHASES DISCOUNT   ACCOUNT NO. 511

Date	Explanation	Post Ref.	Debit	Credit	Balance Debit	Balance Credit

RENT EXPENSE   ACCOUNT NO. 610

Date	Explanation	Post Ref.	Debit	Credit	Balance Debit	Balance Credit

UTILITIES EXPENSE   ACCOUNT NO. 620

Date	Explanation	Post Ref.	Debit	Credit	Balance Debit	Balance Credit

JONES, COMPUTER CENTER
SCHEDULE OF ACCOUNTS PAYABLE
MAY 31, 200X

PROBLEM 10A-4 OR PROBLEM 10B-4

ABBY'S TOY HOUSE
GENERAL JOURNAL

PAGE 1

Date	Account Titles and Description	PR	Dr.	Cr.

PROBLEM 10A-4 OR PROBLEM 10B-4 (CONTINUED)

Date	Account Titles and Description	PR	Dr.	Cr.

PROBLEM 10A-4 OR PROBLEM 10B-4 (CONTINUED)

Date	Account Titles and Description	PR	Dr.	Cr.

PROBLEM A-4 OR PROBLEM B-4 (CONTINUED)

Date	Account Titles and Description	PR	Dr.	Cr.

PROBLEM A-4 OR PROBLEM B-4 (CONTINUED)

Date	Account Titles and Description	PR	Dr.	Cr.

PROBLEM 10A-4 OR PROBLEM 10B-4 (CONTINUED)

(4)

ABBY'S TOY HOUSE
SCHEDULE OF ACCOUNTS RECEIVABLE
MARCH 31, 200X

(4)

ABBY'S TOY HOUSE
SCHEDULE OF ACCOUNTS PAYABLE
MARCH 31, 200X

PROBLEM 10A-4 OR PROBLEM 10B-4 (CONTINUED)

ACCOUNTS PAYABLE SUBSIDIARY LEDGER

NAME MINNIE KATZ

ADDRESS 87 GARFIELD AVE., REVERE, MA 01245

Date		Explanation	Post Ref.	Debit	Credit	Cr. Balance

NAME SAM KATZ GARAGE

ADDRESS 22 REGIS RD., BOSTON, MA 01950

Date		Explanation	Post Ref.	Debit	Credit	Cr. Balance

NAME EARL MILLER CO.

ADDRESS 22 RETTER ST., SAN DIEGO, CA 01211

Date		Explanation	Post Ref.	Debit	Credit	Cr. Balance

NAME WOODY SMITH

ADDRESS 2 SPRING ST., WEERS, ND 02118

Date		Explanation	Post Ref.	Debit	Credit	Cr. Balance

PROBLEM 10A-4 OR PROBLEM 10B-4 (CONTINUED)

ACCOUNTS RECEIVABLE SUBSIDIARY LEDGER

NAME   BILL BURTON

ADDRESS   24 RYAN RD., BUIKE, OH 02183

Date	Explanation	Post Ref.	Debit	Credit	Dr. Balance

NAME   BONNIE FLOW CO.

ADDRESS   2 SMITH RD., DALLAS, TX 22210

Date	Explanation	Post Ref.	Debit	Credit	Dr. Balance

NAME   JIM REX

ADDRESS   1 SCHOOL ST., CLEVELAND, OH 22441

Date	Explanation	Post Ref.	Debit	Credit	Dr. Balance

PROBLEM 10A-4 OR PROBLEM 10B-4 (CONTINUED)

NAME   AMY ROSE

ADDRESS   18 VEEK RD., CHESTER, CT 80111

Date		Explanation	Post Ref.	Debit	Credit	Dr. Balance

GENERAL LEDGER

CASH   ACCOUNT NO. <u>110</u>

Date		Explanation	Post Ref.	Debit	Credit	Balance Debit	Balance Credit

PROBLEM 10A-4 OR PROBLEM 10B-4 (CONTINUED)

ACCOUNTS RECEIVABLE   ACCOUNT NO. 112

Date	Explanation	Post Ref.	Debit	Credit	Balance Debit	Balance Credit

PREPAID RENT   ACCOUNT NO. 112

Date	Explanation	Post Ref.	Debit	Credit	Balance Debit	Balance Credit

DELIVERY TRUCK   ACCOUNT NO. 121

Date	Explanation	Post Ref.	Debit	Credit	Balance Debit	Balance Credit

PROBLEM 10A-4 OR PROBLEM 10B-4 (CONTINUED)

ACCOUNTS PAYABLE   **ACCOUNT NO. 210**

Date	Explanation	Post Ref.	Debit	Credit	Balance Debit	Balance Credit

A. ELLEN, CAPITAL   **ACCOUNT NO. 310**

Date	Explanation	Post Ref.	Debit	Credit	Balance Debit	Balance Credit

TOY SALES   **ACCOUNT NO. 410**

Date	Explanation	Post Ref.	Debit	Credit	Balance Debit	Balance Credit

PROBLEM 10A-4 OR PROBLEM 10B-4 (CONTINUED)

SALES RETURNS AND ALLOWANCES   ACCOUNT NO. 412

Date		Explanation	Post Ref.	Debit	Credit	Balance Debit	Balance Credit

SALES DISCOUNTS   ACCOUNT NO. 414

Date		Explanation	Post Ref.	Debit	Credit	Balance Debit	Balance Credit

TOY PURCHASES   ACCOUNT NO. 510

Date		Explanation	Post Ref.	Debit	Credit	Balance Debit	Balance Credit

PURCHASES RETURNS AND ALLOWANCES   ACCOUNT NO. 512

Date		Explanation	Post Ref.	Debit	Credit	Balance Debit	Balance Credit

PROBLEM 10A-4 OR PROBLEM 10B-4 (CONCLUDED)

PURCHASES DISCOUNT   ACCOUNT NO. 514

Date		Explanation	Post Ref.	Debit	Credit	Balance	
						Debit	Credit

SALARIES EXPENSE   ACCOUNT NO. 610

Date		Explanation	Post Ref.	Debit	Credit	Balance	
						Debit	Credit

CLEANING EXPENSE   ACCOUNT NO. 612

Date		Explanation	Post Ref.	Debit	Credit	Balance	
						Debit	Credit

PROBLEM 10A-5 OR PROBLEM 10B-5

Date		Account Titles and Description	PR			Dr.				Cr.	

PROBLEM 10A-5 OR PROBLEM 10B-5 (CONTINUED)

PAGE 4

Date	Account Titles and Description	PR	Dr.	Cr.

CHAPTER 10
SUMMARY PRACTICE TEST
PURCHASES AND CASH PAYMENTS

Part I Instructions

Fill in the blank(s) to complete the statement.

1. F.O.B. shipping point means the _____ covers the shipping cost.

2. Purchases are categorized as _____.

3. The Purchases account has a _____ balance.

4. Purchases are defined as merchandise for _____ to customers.

5. The accounts payable subsidiary ledger represents a potential _____ of cash.

6. The controlling account in the general ledger for the accounts payable subsidiary ledger is called _____ _____.

7. The accounts payable subsidiary ledger would be recorded _____.

8. The balance in the Accounts Payable controlling account should be equal to the sum of the accounts payable ledger accounts _____ _____ _____ _____.

9. In perpetual inventory, purchases are recorded _____ _____.

10. The ✔ in the reference column indicates that the _____ _____ _____ _____ has been updated.

11. A _____ _____ that is issued means the buyer owes less money, as merchandise is being returned or an allowance received.

12. A debit memorandum issued or a credit memorandum received results in a _____ to Accounts Payable and a credit to Purchases, Returns and Allowances.

13. List price - net price = _____ _____ amount.

14. The accounts payable ledger is listed in _____ _____.

15. Purchases Returns and Allowances is increased by a _____.

16. Cost of goods sold is classified as a _____.

17. In a perpetual inventory system, freight is recorded in the _____ _____ account.

18. Purchases Discounts is increased by _____.

19. A _____ _____ provides the purchasing department the information to then prepare a purchase order.

20. A _____ _____ is made out after a company inspects received shipments.

Part II

Complete the following table:

	Account Title	CAT	↑ ↓	Temp Financial Statement
1.				
2.				
3.				
4.				
5.				
6.				
7.				
8.				
9.				
10.				

Part III Instructions

Answer true or false to the following statements.

1. F.O.B. shipping point means buyer is responsible to cover shipping costs.
2. The purchases account is a contra-cost of goods sold account.
3. Purchases Discounts are the result of paying for equipment within the discount period.
4. F.O.B. Destination means the seller is responsible to cover shipping costs.
5. Purchases Discounts are taken on freight.
6. Merchandise inventory is an asset.
7. Cost of goods sold is a cost.
8. The balance in Accounts Payable, the controlling account, will be equal to the sum of the accounts receivable subsidiary ledger at the end of the month.
9. A purchase order is completed after the purchase requisition.
10. On receiving a purchase order, the seller may issue a sales invoice.
11. The normal balance of Purchases Discount is a debit balance.
12. The seller will often issue a debit memorandum to the buyer.
13. Cost of goods sold is used in a periodic inventory system.
14. Returned equipment by a buyer results in a change in Purchases Returns and Allowances.
15. Trade discounts do not occur because of early payments of one's bills.
16. A seller's sales discount on purchases is the buyers purchases discount.
17. Buying of equipment on account is only recorded in the general ledger.
18. On receiving a debit memorandum, the seller will issue a credit memorandum.
19. Returns in a perpetual accounting system are recorded in the merchandise inventory account.
20. Purchases are contra costs.

CHAPTER 10
SOLUTIONS TO SUMMARY PRACTICE TEST

Part I

1.	buyer (purchaser)	11.	debit memorandum
2.	cost	12.	debit
3.	debit	13.	trade discount
4.	resale	14.	alphabetical order
5.	outflow	15.	credit
6.	accounts payable	16.	cost
7.	daily	17.	merchandise inventory
8.	at end of month	18.	credits
9.	merchandise inventory	19.	purchase requisition
10.	accounts payable subsidiary ledger	20.	receiving report

Part II

1.	cost	Dr	Cr
2.	contra cost	Cr	Dr
3.	asset	Dr	Cr
4.	cost	Dr	Cr
5.	expense	Dr	Cr
6.	liability	Cr	Cr
7.	contra cost	Cr	Dr
8.	asset	Dr	Cr
9.	asset	Dr	Cr
10.	contra revenue	Dr	Cr

Part III

1.	true	11.	false
2.	false	12.	false
3.	false	13.	false
4.	true	14.	false
5.	false	15.	true
6.	true	16.	true
7.	true	17.	false
8.	false	18.	true
9.	true	19.	true
10.	true	20.	false

CONTINUING PROBLEM FOR CHAPTER 10

SANCHEZ COMPUTER CENTER
GENERAL JOURNAL

PAGE 5

Date	Account Titles and Description	PR	Dr.	Cr.

PARTIAL GENERAL LEDGER

CASH   ACCOUNT NO. 1000

Date		Explanation	Post Ref.	Debit	Credit	Balance Debit	Balance Credit
2/1	0X	Balance forward	✔			15 1 1 6 65	

SUPPLIES   ACCOUNT NO. 1030

Date		Explanation	Post Ref.	Debit	Credit	Balance Debit	Balance Credit
2/1	0X	Balance forward	✔			1 3 2 00	

MERCHANDISE INVENTORY   ACCOUNT NO. 1040

Date		Explanation	Post Ref.	Debit	Credit	Balance Debit	Balance Credit

PREPAID RENT   ACCOUNT NO. 1025

Date		Explanation	Post Ref.	Debit	Credit	Balance Debit	Balance Credit
2/1	0X	Balance forward	✓			1 6 0 0 00	

ACCOUNTS PAYABLE   ACCOUNT NO. 2000

Date		Explanation	Post Ref.	Debit	Credit	Balance Debit	Balance Credit
2/1	0X	Balance forward	✓				2 0 5 0 00

PURCHASES   ACCOUNT NO. 6000

Date		Explanation	Post Ref.	Debit	Credit	Balance Debit	Balance Credit

PURCHASE RETURNS AND ALLOWANCES   ACCOUNT NO. 6010

Date		Explanation	Post Ref.	Debit	Credit	Balance Debit	Balance Credit

PURCHASE DISCOUNTS   ACCOUNT NO. 6020

Date		Explanation	Post Ref.	Debit	Credit	Balance Debit	Balance Credit

SANCHEZ COMPUTER CENTER
SCHEDULE OF ACCOUNTS PAYABLE
2/28/0X

ACCOUNTS PAYABLE SUBSIDIARY LEDGER

NAME   MULTI SYSTEMS   # 6A3

ADDRESS   1919 MORAN ST., ANAHEIM, CA 92606

Date		Explanation	Post Ref.	Debit	Credit	Cr. Balance
2/1	0X	Balance forward	✔			4 5 0 00

NAME   OFFICE DEPOT   # 6A4

ADDRESS   460 ESCONDIDO BLVD., ESCONDIDO, CA 92025

Date		Explanation	Post Ref.	Debit	Credit	Cr. Balance
2/1	0X	Balance forward	✔			5 0 00

NAME   SAN DIEGO ELECTRIC   # 6A5

ADDRESS   606 INDUSTRIAL ST., SAN DIEGO, CA 92121

Date		Explanation	Post Ref.	Debit	Credit	Cr. Balance

NAME   PACIFIC BELL   # 6A6

ADDRESS   101 BELL AVE., SAN DIEGO, CA 92101

Date		Explanation	Post Ref.	Debit	Credit	Cr. Balance
2/1	0X	Balance forward	✔			1 5 0 00

NAME   COMPUTER CONNECTION   # 6A7

ADDRESS   1020 WIL LANE, LOS ANGELES, CA 92405

Date		Explanation	Post Ref.	Debit	Credit	Cr. Balance

NAME　　SYSTEMS DESIGN FURNITURE　　　　　　　　　　　　　　**# 6A8**

ADDRESS　　2070 FIRST ST., SAN DIEGO, CA 92101

Date		Explanation	Post Ref.	Debit					Credit					Cr. Balance				
2/1	0X	Balance forward	✔											1	4	0	0	00

PREPARING A WORKSHEET FOR A MERCHANDISE COMPANY

SELF-REVIEW QUIZ 11-1

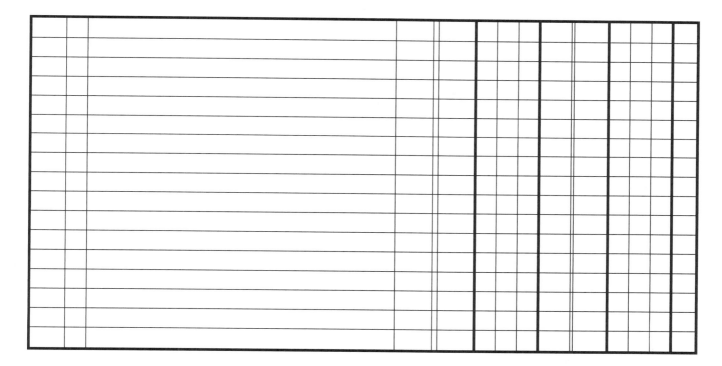

SELF-REVIEW QUIZ 11-2

Use a blank fold-out worksheet located at the end of this text.

FORMS FOR DEMONSTRATION CLASSROOM PROBLEMS SET A OR SET B

1.											
2.											

3.   A. _____   E. _____

       B. _____   F. _____

       C. _____

       D. _____

4.   _____

     _____

     _____

     _____

     _____

     _____

     _____

5.

   A. _____ B. _____ C. _____ D. _____ E. _____ F. _____

FORMS FOR EXERCISES

11-1.

A. _____

B. _____

_____

C. _____

D. _____

E. _____

F. _____

G. _____

H. _____

11-2.

A. _____

_____

B. _____

_____

C. _____

_____

D. _____

_____

_____

11-3.

Accounts Affected	Category	↑ ↓	Rules

11-4.

A. _____

B. _____

C. _____

11-5.

Use a blank fold-out worksheet located at the end of this text.

END OF CHAPTER PROBLEMS

PROBLEM 11A-1 OR PROBLEM 11B-1

A.	
B.	
C.	
D.	

PROBLEM 11A-2 OR PROBLEM 11B-2;
PROBLEM 11A-3 OR PROBLEM 11B-3;
PROBLEM 11A-4 OR PROBLEM 11B-4
Use blank fold-out worksheets located at the end of this text.

CHAPTER 11
SUMMARY PRACTICE TEST:
PREPARING THE WORKSHEET
FOR A MERCHANDISE COMPANY

Part I Instructions

Fill in the blank(s) to complete the statement.

1. The _____ _____ system doesn't keep a continual track of the quantity and cost of the inventory on hand.

2. In the periodic inventory sytsem, all purchases of merchandise during the period is recorded in the _____ account.

3. A continuous record of inventory is kept in a _____ _____ system.

4. When using the periodic system, _____ _____ will remain unchanged.

5. _____ _____ represents a liability on the balance sheet and records money received for a sale or service not yet performed.

6. Freight-in is _____ to the cost of goods sold.

7. Net Sales less Cost of Goods Sold equals _____ _____.

8. _____ _____ equals Gross Sales less Sales Discounts and Sales Returns and Allowances.

9. Net Purchases equals Purchases less _____ _____ and _____ _____ _____ _____.

10. An _____ _____ helps calculate ending inventory.

11. Ending inventory is _____ from the cost of goods available for sale.

12. Net purchases are _____ to Beginning Inventory to get the cost of goods available for sale.

13. Gross Profit less _____ equals Net Income.

14. Purchase discounts _____ the total cost of merchandise sold.

15. Beginning inventory at the end of the period is assumed to be _____, and thus a _____.

16. The ending inventory of one period becomes the _____ _____ next period.

17. Ending inventory represents goods not _____.

18. The inventory account is _____ at the end of the period.

19. Purchases are increased by a _____.

20. Sales returns and allowances are used in calculating _____ _____.

21. Beginning Inventory plus Net Purchases equals _____ _____ _____ _____ _____ _____.

22. Beginning Inventory and Ending Inventory are never _____ on the worksheet.

Part II Instructions

Answer true or false to the following statements.

1. Unearned Revenue is an asset.
2. Perpetual inventory doesn't keep a continuous record of inventory.
3. Purchases reduce cost of goods sold.
4. Freight-in is subtracted from cost of good sold.
5. Figures for Beginning and Ending Inventory are combined on the work sheet.
6. A periodic system is used by companies with low volume and high unit prices.
7. Merchandise Inventory is a liability.
8. Unearned Revenue is a liability on the income statement.
9. Inventory is always taken 10 times per year.
10. Purchases replace ending inventory in a periodic system.
11. A trial balance may be placed directly on a worksheet.
12. The adjustment process updates the inventory account.
13. A post-closing trial balance has no temporary accounts.
14. Sales Discounts is a permanent account.
15. Gross sales are located on the balance sheet.
16. The Sales Returns and Allowances account has a normal balance of a credit.
17. Ending inventory of one period is the beginning inventory of the following period.
18. Net income always means cash.
19. Ending inventory increases cost of goods sold.
20. Net purchases is always the same as total purchases.
21. Gross profit plus expenses equals net income.
22. Unearned Storage Fees is a liability.
23. Merchandise inventory that is sold is assumed to be a cost.
24. Accumulated Depreciation is increased by a debit.
25. Merchandise Inventory can never be listed on a trial balance.
26. Ending Merchandise Inventory can only be found on a balance sheet.
27. The amount of rent expired is used in the adjustment process.
28. Adjustments help update individual ledger accounts.
29. Purchases Returns and Allowances is found on a balance sheet.
30. Beginning Merchandise Inventory found on the balance sheet from the prior period will also be placed in the cost of goods sold section of the balance sheet.
31. Sales always means cash received.
32. Ending Merchandise Inventory of the current period is found only on the balance sheet.
33. Purchases adds to the cost of goods sold.
34. Purchases discounts reduce the cost of purchases on the balance sheet.
35. Beginning inventory can never be assumed sold by the end of a period.

36. Ending inventory in one period becomes beginning inventory for the next two periods.

37. The ending inventory may be calculated from an inventory sheet.

38. Income Summary is used in the adjustment of merchandise inventory.

39. Ending inventory not sold is only placed in the credit column of the balance sheet section on the worksheet.

40. Purchases Discount is recorded in the credit column of the income statement section on the worksheet.

41. Gross profit and net income mean the same.

42. All companies must give sales discounts.

43. A merchandise company does not need a cost of goods sold section on the income statement.

44. Cost of goods available to sell less ending inventory equals cost of goods not sold.

SOLUTIONS TO SUMMARY PRACTICE TEST

Part I

1. periodic inventory

2. Purchases

3. perpetual inventory

4. beginning inventory

5. Unearned Revenue

6. added

7. Gross Profit

8. Net sales

9. Purchases Discounts, Purchases Returns and Allowances

10. Inventory sheet (record)

11. Subtracted

12. added

13. Expenses

14. reduce

15. sold, cost

16. begining inventory

17. sold

18. adjusted

19. debit

20. net sales

21. Cost of Goods Available for Sale

22. combined

Part II

1.	false	**12.**	true	**23.**	true	**34.**	false
2.	false	**13.**	true	**24.**	false	**35.**	false
3.	false	**14.**	false	**25.**	false	**36.**	false
4.	false	**15.**	false	**26.**	false	**37.**	true
5.	false	**16.**	false	**27.**	true	**38.**	true
6.	false	**17.**	true	**28.**	true	**39.**	false
7.	false	**18.**	false	**29.**	false	**40.**	true
8.	false	**19.**	false	**30.**	false	**41.**	false
9.	false	**20.**	false	**31.**	false	**42.**	false
10.	false	**21.**	false	**32.**	false	**43.**	false
11.	true	**22.**	true	**33.**	true	**44.**	false

CONTINUING PROBLEM FOR CHAPTER 11

Use blank fold-out worksheet located at the end of this text.

COMPLETION OF THE ACCOUNTING CYCLE FOR A MERCHANDISE COMPANY

12

Name _____ Class _____ Date _____

SELF-REVIEW QUIZ 12-1

(1)

_____

_____

_____

Name _____ Class _____ Date _____

(2)

Name _____ Class _____ Date _____

(3)

_____
_____
_____

SELF-REVIEW QUIZ 12-2

GENERAL JOURNAL PAGE 2

Date		Account Titles and Description	PR		Dr.			Cr.	

SELF-REVIEW QUIZ 12-3

Situation 1

Situation 2

Situation 3

FORMS FOR DEMONSTRATION PROBLEMS SET A OR SET B

1.

_____
_____
_____
_____

2.

_____
_____
_____
_____

3.

_____
_____
_____
_____

4. A. _____   F. _____
    B. _____   G. _____
    C. _____   H. _____
    D. _____   I. _____
    E. _____   J. _____

5.

FORMS FOR EXERCISES

12-1.

COST OF GOODS SOLD

Merchandise Inv. 12/01/X1	_____
Purchases	_____
Less: Purchases Disc.	_____
Purch. R. & A.	_____
	_____
Net Purchases	_____
Add: Freight-in	_____
Net Cost of Purchases	_____
Cost of Goods Available for Sale	_____
Less: Merchandise Inv. 12/31/X1	_____
Cost of Goods Sold	_____

12-2.

A. _____

B. _____

C. _____

D. _____

E. _____

F. _____

G. _____

12-3.

EXERCISES (CONTINUED)

12-4.

A. SLOW COMPANY
BALANCE SHEET
DECEMBER 31, 200X

12-5.

(A)

Salaries Expense   Salaries Payable

(B)

Salaries Expense   Salaries Expense

(C)

Salaries Expense   Cash

PROBLEM 12A-1 OR PROBLEM 12B-1

RING.COM
INCOME STATEMENT
FOR YEAR ENDED DECEMBER 31, 200X

PROBLEM 12A-2 OR PROBLEM 12B-2

JAMES CO.
STATEMENT OF OWNER'S EQUITY
FOR MONTH ENDED DECEMBER 31, 200X

PROBLEM 12A-2 OR PROBLEM 12B-2 (CONCLUDED)

JAMES CO.
BALANCE SHEET
DECEMBER 31, 200X

PROBLEM 12A-3 OR PROBLEM 12B-3

Use a blank fold-out worksheet located at the end of this text.

JAY'S SUPPLIES
INCOME STATEMENT
FOR YEAR ENDED DECEMBER 31, 200X

PROBLEM 12A-3 OR PROBLEM 12B-3 (CONTINUED)

JAY'S SUPPLIES
STATEMENT OF OWNER'S EQUITY
FOR MONTH ENDED DECEMBER 31, 200X

PROBLEM 12A-3 OR PROBLEM 12B-3 (CONTINUED)

JAY'S SUPPLIES
BALANCE SHEET
DECEMBER 31, 200X

PROBLEM 12A-3 OR PROBLEM 12B-3 (CONTINUED)

GENERAL JOURNAL

Date		Account Titles and Description	PR	Dr.	Cr.

PROBLEM 12A-3 OR PROBLEM 12B-3 (CONCLUDED)

GENERAL JOURNAL

PAGE 3

Date	Account Titles and Description	PR	Dr.	Cr.

PROBLEM 12A-4 OR PROBLEM 12B-4

Use a blank fold-out worksheet located at the end of this text.

CALLAHAN LUMBER
INCOME STATEMENT
FOR YEAR ENDED DECEMBER 31, 200X

PROBLEM 12A-4 OR PROBLEM 12B-4 (CONTINUED)

Use a blank fold-out worksheet located at the end of this text.

CALLAHAN LUMBER
STATEMENT OF OWNER'S EQUITY
FOR YEAR ENDED DECEMBER 31, 200X

PROBLEM 12A-4 OR PROBLEM 12B-4 (CONTINUED)

CALLAHAN LUMBER
BALANCE SHEET
DECEMBER 31, 200X

PROBLEM 12A-4 OR PROBLEM 12B-4 (CONTINUED)

GENERAL JOURNAL

PAGE 2

Date		Account Titles and Description	PR		Dr.			Cr.		

PROBLEM 12A-4 OR PROBLEM 12B-4 (CONTINUED)

CALLAHAN LUMBER
GENERAL LEDGER

CASH   **ACCOUNT NO. 110**

Date	Explanation	Post Ref.	Debit	Credit	Balance Debit	Balance Credit

ACCOUNTS RECEIVABLE   **ACCOUNT NO. 111**

Date	Explanation	Post Ref.	Debit	Credit	Balance Debit	Balance Credit

MERCHANDISE INVENTORY   **ACCOUNT NO. 112**

Date	Explanation	Post Ref.	Debit	Credit	Balance Debit	Balance Credit

LUMBER SUPPLIES   **ACCOUNT NO. 112**

Date	Explanation	Post Ref.	Debit	Credit	Balance Debit	Balance Credit

PROBLEM 12A-4 OR PROBLEM 12B-4 (CONTINUED)

PREPAID INSURANCE   ACCOUNT NO. 114

Date		Explanation	Post Ref.	Debit	Credit	Balance	
						Debit	Credit

LUMBER EQUIPMENT   ACCOUNT NO. 121

Date		Explanation	Post Ref.	Debit	Credit	Balance	
						Debit	Credit

ACCUMULATED DEPRECIATION, LUMBER EQUIPMENT   ACCOUNT NO. 122

Date		Explanation	Post Ref.	Debit	Credit	Balance	
						Debit	Credit

ACCOUNTS PAYABLE   ACCOUNT NO. 220

Date		Explanation	Post Ref.	Debit	Credit	Balance	
						Debit	Credit

WAGES PAYABLE   ACCOUNT NO. 221

Date		Explanation	Post Ref.	Debit	Credit	Balance	
						Debit	Credit

PROBLEM 12A-4 OR PROBLEM 12B-4 (CONTINUED)

J. CALLAHAN, CAPITAL ACCOUNT NO. 330

Date	Explanation	Post Ref.	Debit	Credit	Balance Debit	Balance Credit

J. CALLAHAN, WITHDRAWALS ACCOUNT NO. 331

Date	Explanation	Post Ref.	Debit	Credit	Balance Debit	Balance Credit

INCOME SUMMARY ACCOUNT NO. 332

Date	Explanation	Post Ref.	Debit	Credit	Balance Debit	Balance Credit

SALES ACCOUNT NO. 440

Date	Explanation	Post Ref.	Debit	Credit	Balance Debit	Balance Credit

SALES RETURNS AND ALLOWANCES ACCOUNT NO. 441

Date	Explanation	Post Ref.	Debit	Credit	Balance Debit	Balance Credit

PROBLEM 12A-4 OR PROBLEM 12B-4 (CONTINUED)

PURCHASES   ACCOUNT NO. 550

Date	Explanation	Post Ref.	Debit	Credit	Balance Debit	Balance Credit

PURCHASES DISCOUNT   ACCOUNT NO. 551

Date	Explanation	Post Ref.	Debit	Credit	Balance Debit	Balance Credit

PURCHASES RETURNS AND ALLOWANCES   ACCOUNT NO. 552

Date	Explanation	Post Ref.	Debit	Credit	Balance Debit	Balance Credit

WAGES EXPENSE   ACCOUNT NO. 660

Date	Explanation	Post Ref.	Debit	Credit	Balance Debit	Balance Credit

ADVERTISING EXPENSE   ACCOUNT NO. 661

Date	Explanation	Post Ref.	Debit	Credit	Balance Debit	Balance Credit

PROBLEM 12A-4 OR PROBLEM 12B-4 (CONTINUED)

RENT EXPENSE   ACCOUNT NO. 662

Date	Explanation	Post Ref.	Debit	Credit	Balance Debit	Balance Credit

DEPRECIATION EXPENSE, LUMBER EQUIPMENT   ACCOUNT NO. 663

Date	Explanation	Post Ref.	Debit	Credit	Balance Debit	Balance Credit

LUMBER SUPPLIES EXPENSE   ACCOUNT NO. 664

Date	Explanation	Post Ref.	Debit	Credit	Balance Debit	Balance Credit

INSURANCE EXPENSE   ACCOUNT NO. 665

Date	Explanation	Post Ref.	Debit	Credit	Balance Debit	Balance Credit

PROBLEM 12A-4 OR PROBLEM 12B-4 (CONCLUDED)

CALLAHAN LUMBER
POST-CLOSING TRIAL BALANCE
DECEMBER 31, 200X

	Dr.	Cr.

CHAPTER 12
SUMMARY PRACTICE TEST:
COMPLETION OF THE ACCOUNTING
CYCLE FOR A MERCHANDISE COMPANY

Part I

Fill in the blank(s) to complete the statement.

1. The inside columns for financial reports are used for _____.

2. The fomal income statement uses _____ _____ figures for inventory.

3. The gross profit figure _____ (is/is not) found on the worksheet.

4. _____ expenses are related to the selling activity.

5. _____ _____ are related to the administrative function.

6. _____ _____ could be broken down into selling and administrative expenses.

7. The _____ figure for capital is not found on the worksheet.

8. _____ _____ are cash or other assets that will be converted into cash during the normal operating cycle of the company or one year, whichever is longer.

9. _____ and _____ are long-lived assets used for the production or sale of other assets or services.

10. Debts or obligations that are to be paid with current assets within one year or one operating cycle are called _____ _____ _____.

11. Mortgage Payable is an example of a _____.

12. Ending merchandise inventory is a _____ _____.

13. By the adjusting process, the beginning inventory of the period is transferred to _____ _____.

14. The post-closing trial balance contains no _____ accounts.

15. A reversing entry involves certain _____ entries.

16. Reversing entries are used only if assets are _____ and have no previous balance and liabilities are _____ and have no balance.

Part II Instructions

Match the term in the last column to the definition, example, or phrase in the right column. Be sure to use a letter only once.

_____d_____ 1. EXAMPLE: Equipment
_____ 2. Net Sales-Cost of Goods Sold
_____ 3. Operating Cycle
_____ 4. Subtotalling
_____ 5. Gross Profit-Operating Expenses
_____ 6. Operating Expenses
_____ 7. Temporary Account
_____ 8. FICA Tax Payable-Soc. Sec.
_____ 9. Result of an adjusting entry
_____ 10. Petty Cash
_____ 11. An asset that is adjsuted
_____ 12. Ending Capital
_____ 13. A Liability showing revenue no earned
_____ 14. Unearned training fees

a. Inside columns of financial reports
b. Unearned Revenue
c. Current asset
d. Plant and Equipment
e. Reversing Entry
f. Time Period
g. Net Income
h. Current Liability
i. When earned reduced by a debit
j. Gross Profit
k. Merchandise Inventory
l. Debit Balance
m. Not found on worksheet
n. Income Summary
o. Selling and Administrative

Part III Instructions

Answer true or false to the following statements.

1. Formal statements contain debit and credit columns.
2. Cost of goods sold contains only ending inventory.
3. Net sales less cost of goods sold equals gross profit.
4. Operating expenses can only be administrative.
5. Supplies is part of Plant and Equipment.
6. Unearned Rent is a liability.
7. An operating cycle of a business must be one year.
8. Accumulated Depreciation is a current asset.
9. Long-term liabilities are due within one year.
10. Merchandise Inventory is a temporary account.
11. The normal balance of merchandise inventory is a debit.
12. The post-closing trial balance will not contain any unearned revenue accounts.
13. Ending inventory is closed directly to Capital.
14. Reversing entries cannot be applied to all adjustments.
15. Reversing entries are optional at the end of each month before close of year.
16. Reversing entries switch closing entries on the first day of new period.
17. An adjusting entry with an asset decreasing with no prevouis balance cannot be reversed.
18. Closing entries will update the merchandise inventory account.
19. Beginning merchandise inventory of a period is assumed sold by end of the period.
20. An adjusting entry for Accrued Wages can be reversed.

CHAPTER 12
SOLUTIONS TO SUMMARY PRACTICE TEST

Part I

1. subtotalling
2. two separate
3. not
4. Selling
5. Administrative expenses
6. Operating expenses
7. ending
8. Current assets
9. Plant, Equipment
10. current liabilities
11. long-term liability
12. permanent account
13. Income Summary
14. temporary
15. adjusting
16. increasing, increasing

Part II

1. d
2. j
3. f
4. a
5. g
6. o
7. n
8. h
9. e
10. l
11. k
12. m
13. b
14. i

Part III

1. false
2. false
3. true
4. false
5. false
6. true
7. false
8. false
9. false
10. false
11. true
12. false
13. false
14. true
15. false
16. false
17. true
18. false
19. true
20. true

CONTINUING PROBLEM FOR CHAPTER 12

SANCHEZ COMPUTER CENTER
GENERAL JOURNAL
PAGE 1

Date	Account Titles and Description	PR	Dr.	Cr.

SANCHEZ COMPUTER CENTER
GENERAL LEDGER

CASH   ACCOUNT NO. **1000**

Date		Explanation	Post Ref.	Debit	Credit	Balance Debit	Balance Credit
3/1	0X	Balance forward	✔			12 5 1 6 65	

PETTY CASH   ACCOUNT NO. **1010**

Date		Explanation	Post Ref.	Debit	Credit	Balance Debit	Balance Credit
3/1	0X	Balance forward	✔			1 0 0 00	

ACCOUNTS RECEIVABLE   ACCOUNT NO. **1020**

Date		Explanation	Post Ref.	Debit	Credit	Balance Debit	Balance Credit
3/1	0X	Balance forward	✔			11 9 0 0 00	

PREPAID RENT   ACCOUNT NO. **1025**

Date		Explanation	Post Ref.	Debit	Credit	Balance Debit	Balance Credit
3/1	0X	Balance forward	✔			2 8 0 0 00	

SUPPLIES   ACCOUNT NO. 1030

Date		Explanation	Post Ref.	Debit	Credit	Balance Debit	Balance Credit
3/1	0X	Balance forward	✔			4 3 2 00	

MERCHANDISE INVENTORY   ACCOUNT NO. 1040

Date		Explanation	Post Ref.	Debit	Credit	Balance Debit	Balance Credit

COMPUTER SHOP EQUIPMENT   ACCOUNT NO. 1080

Date		Explanation	Post Ref.	Debit	Credit	Balance Debit	Balance Credit
3/1	0X	Balance forward	✔			3 8 0 0	

ACCUMULATED DEPRECIATION, C.S. EQUIPMENT   ACCOUNT NO. 1081

Date		Explanation	Post Ref.	Debit	Credit	Balance Debit	Balance Credit
3/1	0X	Balance forward	✔				9 9 00

OFFICE EQUIPMENT   ACCOUNT NO. 1090

Date		Explanation	Post Ref.	Debit	Credit	Balance Debit	Balance Credit
3/1	0X	Balance forward	✔			1 0 5 0 00	

ACCUMULATED DEPRECIATION, OFFICE EQUIPMENT   ACCOUNT NO. 1091

Date		Explanation	Post Ref.	Debit	Credit	Balance Debit	Balance Credit
3/1	0X	Balance forward	✔				2 0 00

ACCOUNTS PAYABLE   ACCOUNT NO. 2000

Date		Explanation	Post Ref.	Debit	Credit	Balance Debit	Balance Credit
3/1	0X	Balance forward	✔				2 8 4 0 00

WAGES PAYABLE   ACCOUNT NO. 2010

Date		Explanation	Post Ref.	Debit	Credit	Balance Debit	Balance Credit

FICA S.S. PAYABLE   ACCOUNT NO. 2020

Date		Explanation	Post Ref.	Debit	Credit	Balance Debit	Balance Credit

FICA MEDICARE PAYABLE   ACCOUNT NO. 2030

Date		Explanation	Post Ref.	Debit	Credit	Balance Debit	Balance Credit

FIT PAYABLE ACCOUNT NO. 2040

Date		Explanation	Post Ref.	Debit	Credit	Balance	
						Debit	Credit

SIT PAYABLE ACCOUNT NO. 2050

Date		Explanation	Post Ref.	Debit	Credit	Balance	
						Debit	Credit

FUTA PAYABLE ACCOUNT NO. 2060

Date		Explanation	Post Ref.	Debit	Credit	Balance	
						Debit	Credit

SUTA PAYABLE ACCOUNT NO. 2070

Date		Explanation	Post Ref.	Debit	Credit	Balance	
						Debit	Credit

T. FREEDMAN, CAPITAL ACCOUNT NO. 3000

Date		Explanation	Post Ref.	Debit	Credit	Balance	
						Debit	Credit
3/1	0X	Balance forward	✔				7 4 0 6 00

T. FREEDMAN WITHDRAWALS   ACCOUNT NO. 3010

Date		Explanation	Post Ref.	Debit	Credit	Balance Debit	Balance Credit
3/1	0X	Balance forward	✔			2 0 1 5 00	

INCOME SUMMARY   ACCOUNT NO. 3020

Date		Explanation	Post Ref.	Debit	Credit	Balance Debit	Balance Credit

SERVICE REVENUE   ACCOUNT NO. 4000

Date		Explanation	Post Ref.	Debit	Credit	Balance Debit	Balance Credit
3/1	0X	Balance forward	✔				19 8 0 0 00

SALES   ACCOUNT NO. 4010

Date		Explanation	Post Ref.	Debit	Credit	Balance Debit	Balance Credit
3/1	0X	Balance forward	✔				9 7 0 0 00

GENERAL LEDGER

SALES RETURN AND ALLOWANCES   ACCOUNT NO. <u>4020</u>

Date		Explanation	Post Ref.	Debit	Credit	Balance	
						Debit	Credit
3/1	0X	Balance forward	✔			4 0 0 00	

SALES DISCOUNTS   ACCOUNT NO. <u>4030</u>

Date		Explanation	Post Ref.	Debit	Credit	Balance	
						Debit	Credit
3/1	0X	Balance forward	✔			2 2 0 00	

ADVERTISING EXPENSE   ACCOUNT NO. <u>5010</u>

Date		Explanation	Post Ref.	Debit	Credit	Balance	
						Debit	Credit
3/1	0X	Balance forward	✔			8 0 0 00	

RENT EXPENSE   ACCOUNT NO. <u>5020</u>

Date		Explanation	Post Ref.	Debit	Credit	Balance	
						Debit	Credit

UTILITIES EXPENSE   ACCOUNT NO. <u>5030</u>

Date		Explanation	Post Ref.	Debit	Credit	Balance	
						Debit	Credit
3/1	0X	Balance forward	✔			2 9 0 00	

PHONE EXPENSE   ACCOUNT NO. 5040

Date		Explanation	Post Ref.	Debit	Credit	Balance	
						Debit	Credit
3/1	0X	Balance forward	✔			1 5 0 00	

SUPPLIES EXPENSE   ACCOUNT NO. 5050

Date		Explanation	Post Ref.	Debit	Credit	Balance	
						Debit	Credit

INSURANCE EXPENSE   ACCOUNT NO. 5060

Date		Explanation	Post Ref.	Debit	Credit	Balance	
						Debit	Credit
3/1	0X	Balance forward	✔			1 0 0 00	

POSTAGE EXPENSE   ACCOUNT NO. 5070

Date		Explanation	Post Ref.	Debit	Credit	Balance	
						Debit	Credit
3/1	0X	Balance forward	✔			1 7 5 00	

DEPRECIATION EXPENSE C.S. EQUIPMENT   ACCOUNT NO. 5080

Date		Explanation	Post Ref.	Debit	Credit	Balance	
						Debit	Credit

DEPRECIATION EXPENSE OFFICE EQUIPMENT   ACCOUNT NO. 5090

Date		Explanation	Post Ref.	Debit	Credit	Balance	
						Debit	Credit

MISCELLANEOUS EXPENSE   ACCOUNT NO. 5100

Date		Explanation	Post Ref.	Debit	Credit	Balance	
						Debit	Credit
3/1	0X	Balance forward	✔			1 0 00	

WAGE EXPENSE   ACCOUNT NO. 5110

Date		Explanation	Post Ref.	Debit	Credit	Balance	
						Debit	Credit
3/1	0X	Balance forward	✔			2 0 3 0 00	

PAYROLL TAX EXPENSE   ACCOUNT NO. 5120

Date		Explanation	Post Ref.	Debit	Credit	Balance	
						Debit	Credit
3/1	0X	Balance forward	✔			2 2 6 35	

INTEREST EXPENSE   ACCOUNT NO. 5130

Date		Explanation	Post Ref.	Debit	Credit	Balance	
						Debit	Credit

BAD DEBT EXPENSE   ACCOUNT NO. 5140

Date	Explanation	Post Ref.	Debit	Credit	Balance Debit	Balance Credit

PURCHASES   ACCOUNT NO. 6000

Date		Explanation	Post Ref.	Debit	Credit	Balance Debit	Balance Credit
3/1	0X	Balance forward	✔			9 5 0 00	

PURCHASE RETURNS AND ALLOWANCES   ACCOUNT NO. 6010

Date		Explanation	Post Ref.	Debit	Credit	Balance Debit	Balance Credit
3/1	0X	Balance forward	✔				1 0 0 00

PURCHASE DISCOUNTS   ACCOUNT NO. 6020

Date	Explanation	Post Ref.	Debit	Credit	Balance Debit	Balance Credit

FREIGHT IN   ACCOUNT NO. 6030

Date	Explanation	Post Ref.	Debit	Credit	Balance Debit	Balance Credit

CONTINUING PROBLEM FOR CHAPTER 12

SANCHEZ COMPUTER CENTER
INCOME STATEMENT
FOR THE SIX MONTHS ENDED MARCH 31, 200X

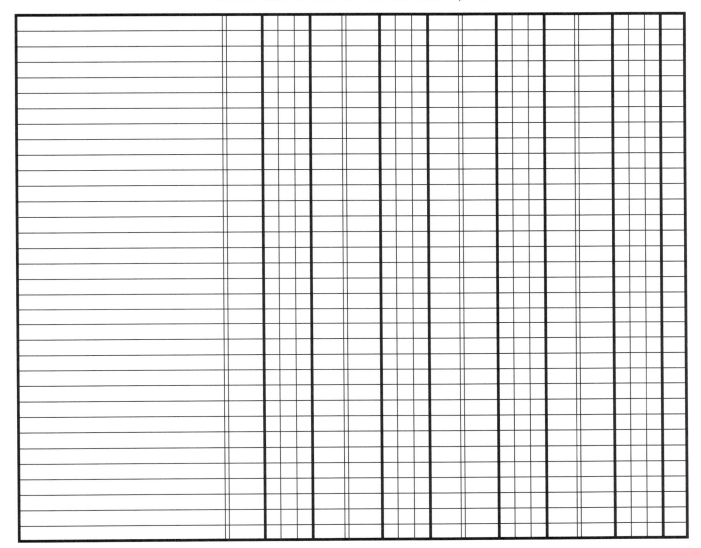

SANCHEZ COMPUTER CENTER
STATEMENT OF OWNER'S EQUITY
FOR THE SIX MONTHS ENDED MARCH 31, 200X

SANCHEZ COMPUTER CENTER
BALANCE SHEET
MARCH 31, 200X

THE CORNER DRESS SHOP
GENERAL JOURNAL

COMPREHENSIVE REVIEW PROBLEM:

Date	Account Titles and Description	PR	Dr.	Cr.

THE CORNER DRESS SHOP

Use a blank fold-out worksheet and the blank payroll register located at the end of this text.

MINI PRACTICE SET (FOR WORKSHEETS, USE FORMS AT END OF TEXT)

THE CORNER DRESS SHOP
GENERAL JOURNAL

PAGE 5

Date	Account Titles and Description	PR	Dr.	Cr.

MINI PRACTICE SET

THE CORNER DRESS SHOP
GENERAL JOURNAL

PAGE 6

Date	Account Titles and Description	PR	Dr.	Cr.

MINI PRACTICE SET

THE CORNER DRESS SHOP
GENERAL JOURNAL

Date		Account Titles and Description	PR	Dr.	Cr.

MINI PRACTICE SET

THE CORNER DRESS SHOP
GENERAL JOURNAL

PAGE 8

Date		Account Titles and Description	PR		Dr.			Cr.	

MINI PRACTICE SET

THE CORNER DRESS SHOP
GENERAL JOURNAL

PAGE 9

Date	Account Titles and Description	PR	Dr.	Cr.

MINI PRACTICE SET

THE CORNER DRESS SHOP
AUXILIARY PETTY CASH RECORD

Date	Voucher No.	Description	Receipts	Payment	Category of Payment					
					Postage Expense	Delivery Expense	Sundry		
							Account	Amount	

MINI PRACTICE SET:

ACCOUNTS PAYABLE SUBSIDIARY LEDGER

NAME   BLEW CO.

Date 190X		Explanation	Post Ref.	Debit	Credit	Credit Balance
MAR	1	Balance	✔			1 9 0 0 00

NAME   JONES CO.

Date 190X		Explanation	Post Ref.	Debit	Credit	Credit Balance

NAME   MOE'S GARAGE

Date 190X		Explanation	Post Ref.	Debit	Credit	Credit Balance

MINI PRACTICE SET

NAME   MORRIS CO.

Date 200X		Explanation	Post Ref.	Debit	Credit	Credit Balance

ACCOUNTS RECEIVABLE SUBSIDIARY LEDGER

NAME   BING CO.

Date 200X		Explanation	Post Ref.	Debit	Credit	Debit Balance
MAR	1	Balance	✔			2 2 0 0 00

NAME   BLEW CO.

Date 200X		Explanation	Post Ref.	Debit	Credit	Debit Balance

MINI PRACTICE SET

NAME   RONALD CO. _____

Date 200X	Explanation	Post Ref.	Debit	Credit	Debit Balance

GENERAL LEDGER

CASH   **ACCOUNT NO. 110**

Date 200X	Explanation	Post Ref.	Debit	Credit	Balance Debit	Balance Credit
MAR 1	Balance	✔			2 2 3 1 90	

MINI PRACTICE SET

ACCOUNTS RECEIVABLE   ACCOUNT NO. 111

Date 200X	Explanation	Post Ref.	Debit	Credit	Balance Debit	Balance Credit
MAR 1	Balance	✔			2 2 0 0 00	

PETTY CASH   ACCOUNT NO. 112

Date 200X	Explanation	Post Ref.	Debit	Credit	Balance Debit	Balance Credit
MAR 1	Balance	✔			3 5 00	

MERCHANDISE INVENTORY   ACCOUNT NO. 114

Date 200X	Explanation	Post Ref.	Debit	Credit	Balance Debit	Balance Credit
MAR 1	Balance	✔			5 6 0 0 00	

Name _____ Class _____ Date _____

MINI PRACTICE SET

PREPAID RENT

ACCOUNT NO. 116

Date 200X		Explanation	Post Ref.	Debit	Credit	Balance	
						Debit	Credit
MAR	1	Balance	✔			1 8 0 0 00	

DELIVERY TRUCK

ACCOUNT NO. 120

Date 200X		Explanation	Post Ref.	Debit	Credit	Balance	
						Debit	Credit
MAR	1	Balance	✔			6 0 0 0 00	

ACCUMULATED DEPRECIATION, TRUCK

ACCOUNT NO. 121

Date 200X		Explanation	Post Ref.	Debit	Credit	Balance	
						Debit	Credit
MAR	1	Balance	✔				1 5 0 0 00

MINI PRACTICE SET

ACCOUNTS PAYABLE   ACCOUNT NO. 210

Date 200X		Explanation	Post Ref.	Debit	Credit	Balance Debit	Balance Credit
MAR	1	Balance	✔				1 9 0 0 00

SALARIES PAYABLE   ACCOUNT NO. 212

Date 200X	Explanation	Post Ref.	Debit	Credit	Balance Debit	Balance Credit

FIT PAYABLE   ACCOUNT NO. 214

Date 200X		Explanation	Post Ref.	Debit	Credit	Balance Debit	Balance Credit
MAR	1	Balance	✔				1 0 1 3 00

MINI PRACTICE SET

FICA-OASDI PAYABLE   ACCOUNT NO. 216

Date 200X	Explanation	Post Ref.	Debit	Credit	Balance Debit	Balance Credit
MAR 1	Balance	✔				1 3 3 9 20

FICA-MEDICARE PAYABLE   ACCOUNT NO. 218

Date 200X	Explanation	Post Ref.	Debit	Credit	Balance Debit	Balance Credit
MAR 1	Balance	✔				3 1 3 20

SIT PAYABLE   ACCOUNT NO. 220

Date 200X	Explanation	Post Ref.	Debit	Credit	Balance Debit	Balance Credit
MAR 1	Balance	✔				7 5 6 00

SUTA TAX PAYABLE   ACCOUNT NO. 222

Date 200X	Explanation	Post Ref.	Debit	Credit	Balance Debit	Balance Credit
MAR 1	Balance	✔				9 7 9 20

FUTA TAX PAYABLE   ACCOUNT NO. 224

Date 200X	Explanation	Post Ref.	Debit	Credit	Balance Debit	Balance Credit
MAR 1	Balance	✔				1 6 3 20

UNEARNED RENT   ACCOUNT NO. 226

Date 200X	Explanation	Post Ref.	Debit	Credit	Balance Debit	Balance Credit
MAR 1	Balance	✔				8 0 0 00

MINI PRACTICE SET

B. LOEB, CAPITAL   ACCOUNT NO. <u>310</u>

Date 200X		Explanation	Post Ref.	Debit	Credit	Balance Debit	Balance Credit
MAR	1	Balance	✔				9 1 0 3 10

B. LOEB, WITHDRAWALS   ACCOUNT NO. <u>320</u>

Date 200X	Explanation	Post Ref.	Debit	Credit	Balance Debit	Balance Credit

INCOME SUMMARY   ACCOUNT NO. <u>330</u>

Date 200X	Explanation	Post Ref.	Debit	Credit	Balance Debit	Balance Credit

SALES   ACCOUNT NO. <u>410</u>

Date 200X	Explanation	Post Ref.	Debit	Credit	Balance Debit	Balance Credit

SALES RETURNS AND ALLOWANCES   ACCOUNT NO. <u>412</u>

Date 200X	Explanation	Post Ref.	Debit	Credit	Balance Debit	Balance Credit

MINI PRACTICE SET

SALES DISCOUINT   ACCOUNT NO. 414

Date 200X	Explanation	Post Ref.	Debit	Credit	Balance Debit	Balance Credit

RENTAL INCOME   ACCOUNT NO. 416

Date 200X	Explanation	Post Ref.	Debit	Credit	Balance Debit	Balance Credit

PURCHASES   ACCOUNT NO. 510

Date 200X	Explanation	Post Ref.	Debit	Credit	Balance Debit	Balance Credit

PURCHASES RETURNS AND ALLOWANCES   ACCOUNT NO. 512

Date 200X	Explanation	Post Ref.	Debit	Credit	Balance Debit	Balance Credit

PURCHASES DISCOUNT   ACCOUNT NO. 514

Date 200X	Explanation	Post Ref.	Debit	Credit	Balance Debit	Balance Credit

MINI PRACTICE SET

SALES SALARY EXPENSE   ACCOUNT NO. 610

Date 200X	Explanation	Post Ref.	Debit	Credit	Balance	
					Debit	Credit

OFFICE SALARY EXPENSE   ACCOUNT NO. 611

Date 200X	Explanation	Post Ref.	Debit	Credit	Balance	
					Debit	Credit

PAYROLL TAX EXPENSE   ACCOUNT NO. 612

Date 200X	Explanation	Post Ref.	Debit	Credit	Balance	
					Debit	Credit

CLEANING EXPENSE   ACCOUNT NO. 614

Date 200X	Explanation	Post Ref.	Debit	Credit	Balance	
					Debit	Credit

DEPRECIATION EXPENSE, TRUCK   ACCOUNT NO. 616

Date 200X	Explanation	Post Ref.	Debit	Credit	Balance	
					Debit	Credit

MINI PRACTICE SET

RENT EXPENSE   ACCOUNT NO. 618

Date 200X		Explanation	Post Ref.	Debit	Credit	Balance	
						Debit	Credit

POSTAGE EXPENSE   ACCOUNT NO. 620

Date 200X		Explanation	Post Ref.	Debit	Credit	Balance	
						Debit	Credit

DELIVERY EXPENSE   ACCOUNT NO. 622

Date 200X		Explanation	Post Ref.	Debit	Credit	Balance	
						Debit	Credit

MISCELLANEOUS EXPENSE   ACCOUNT NO. 624

Date 200X		Explanation	Post Ref.	Debit	Credit	Balance	
						Debit	Credit

MINI PRACTICE SET

THE CORNER DRESS SHOP
SCHEDULE OF ACCOUNTS RECEIVABLE
MARCH 31, 200X

THE CORNER DRESS SHOP
SCHEDULE OF ACCOUNTS PAYABLE
MARCH 31, 200X

MINI PRACTICE SET

THE CORNER DRESS SHOP
INCOME STATEMENT
FOR MONTH ENDED MARCH 31, 200X

MINI PRACTICE SET

THE CORNER DRESS SHOP
STATEMENT OF OWNER'S EQUITY
FOR MONTH ENDED MARCH 31, 200X

MINI PRACTICE SET

THE CORNER DRESS SHOP
BALANCE SHEET
MARCH 31, 200X

MINI PRACTICE SET

THE CORNER DRESS SHOP
POST-CLOSING TRIAL BALANCE
MARCH 31, 200X

Name _____ Class _____ Date _____

Form **941 for 200X:** Employer's QUARTERLY Federal Tax Return

990106

(Rev. January 2006)
Department of the Treasury — Internal Revenue Service

OMB No. 1545-0029

(EIN)
Employer identification number   ☐☐ – ☐☐☐☐☐☐☐

Name *(not your trade name)* _____

Trade name *(if any)* _____

Address _____
        Number   Street   Suite or room number
        _____
        City   State   ZIP code

Report for this Quarter ...
(Check one.)

☐ **1:** January, February, March

☐ **2:** April, May, June

☐ **3:** July, August, September

☐ **4:** October, November, December

Read the separate instructions before you fill out this form. Please type or print within the boxes.

Part 1: Answer these questions for this quarter.

1 Number of employees who received wages, tips, or other compensation for the pay period including: *Mar. 12* (Quarter 1), *June 12* (Quarter 2), *Sept. 12* (Quarter 3), *Dec. 12* (Quarter 4)   1 [   ]

2 Wages, tips, and other compensation . . . .   2 [.]

3 Total income tax withheld from wages, tips, and other compensation . . . .   3 [.]

4 If no wages, tips, and other compensation are subject to social security or Medicare tax . .   ☐ Check and go to line 6.

5 Taxable social security and Medicare wages and tips:

	Column 1		Column 2
5a Taxable social security wages	[.]	× .124 =	[.]
5b Taxable social security tips	[.]	× .124 =	[.]
5c Taxable Medicare wages & tips	[.]	× .029 =	[.]

5d Total social security and Medicare taxes (*Column 2,* lines 5a + 5b + 5c = line 5d) . .   5d [.]

6 Total taxes before adjustments (lines 3 + 5d = line 6) . . . .   6 [.]

7 TAX ADJUSTMENTS (Read the instructions for line 7 before completing lines 7a through 7h.):

7a Current quarter's fractions of cents . . . .   [.]

7b Current quarter's sick pay . . . .   [.]

7c Current quarter's adjustments for tips and group-term life insurance   [.]

7d Current year's income tax withholding (attach Form 941c) . . .   [.]

7e Prior quarters' social security and Medicare taxes (attach Form 941c)   [.]

7f Special additions to federal income tax (attach Form 941c) . . .   [.]

7g Special additions to social security and Medicare (attach Form 941c)   [.]

7h TOTAL ADJUSTMENTS (Combine all amounts: lines 7a through 7g.) . . . . . .   7h [.]

8 Total taxes after adjustments (Combine lines 6 and 7h.) . . . .   8 [.]

9 Advance earned income credit (EIC) payments made to employees . . . .   9 [.]

10 Total taxes after adjustment for advance EIC (line 8 – line 9 = line 10) . . . . . .   10 [.]

11 Total deposits for this quarter, including overpayment applied from a prior quarter . . .   11 [.]

12 Balance due (If line 10 is more than line 11, write the difference here.) . . . .   12 [.]
Make checks payable to *United States Treasury.*

13 Overpayment (If line 11 is more than line 10, write the difference here.)   [.]   Check one ☐ Apply to next return.
                                                                                            ☐ Send a refund.

▶ You **MUST** fill out both pages of this form and **SIGN** it.

Next ➡

For Privacy Act and Paperwork Reduction Act Notice, see the back of the Payment Voucher.   Cat. No. 17001Z   Form **941** (Rev. 1-2006)

990206

Name *(not your trade name)* | Employer identification number (EIN)

Part 2: Tell us about your deposit schedule and tax liability for this quarter.

If you are unsure about whether you are a monthly schedule depositor or a semiweekly schedule depositor, see *Pub. 15 (Circular E)*, section 11.

14 [ ][ ] Write the state abbreviation for the state where you made your deposits OR write "MU" if you made your deposits in *multiple* states.

15 Check one: [ ] Line 10 is less than $2,500. Go to Part 3.

[ ] You were a monthly schedule depositor for the entire quarter. Fill out your tax liability for each month. Then go to Part 3.

Tax liability: Month 1 [_____ .]

Month 2 [_____ .]

Month 3 [_____ .]

Total liability for quarter [_____ .] Total must equal line 10.

[ ] You were a semiweekly schedule depositor for any part of this quarter. Fill out *Schedule B (Form 941): Report of Tax Liability for Semiweekly Schedule Depositors*, and attach it to this form.

Part 3: Tell us about your business. If a question does NOT apply to your business, leave it blank.

16 If your business has closed or you stopped paying wages . . . . [ ] Check here, and

enter the final date you paid wages [__ / __ / __] .

17 If you are a seasonal employer and you do not have to file a return for every quarter of the year . . [ ] Check here.

Part 4: May we speak with your third-party designee?

Do you want to allow an employee, a paid tax preparer, or another person to discuss this return with the IRS? See the instructions for details.

[ ] Yes. Designee's name [_____]

Phone (___) ___ – ___   Personal Identification Number (PIN) [ ][ ][ ][ ][ ]

[ ] No.

Part 5: Sign here. You MUST fill out both sides of this form and SIGN it.

Under penalties of perjury, I declare that I have examined this return, including accompanying schedules and statements, and to the best of my knowledge and belief, it is true, correct, and complete.

X Sign your name here [_____]

Print name and title [_____]

Date [__ / __ / __]   Phone (___) ___ – ___

Part 6: For PAID preparers only *(optional)*

Paid Preparer's Signature [_____]

Firm's name [_____]

Address [_____]   EIN [_____]

[_____]   ZIP code [_____]

Date [__ / __ / __]   Phone (___) ___ – ___   SSN/PTIN [_____]

[ ] Check if you are self-employed.

SG-423